I Liked You Better
Before I Knew You So Well

I Liked You Better
Before I Knew You So Well

James Allen Hall

I Liked You Better Before I Knew You So Well
FIRST EDITION

Copyright © 2017 James Allen Hall
All rights reserved
Printed in the United States of America

ISBN 978·0·9963167·7·4
DESIGN ≈ SEVY PEREZ
Text in Brandon Grotesque and Adobe Caslon Pro

COVER IMAGE
"Maciek Mika in Munich Rephotographed
in Berlin 2009," by Tim Hailand
In memory of Maciek (1983–2014)

This book is published by the

Cleveland State University Poetry Center
csupoetrycenter.com
2121 Euclid Avenue, Cleveland, Ohio 44115-2214

and is distributed by

SPD / Small Press Distribution, Inc.
spdbooks.org
1341 Seventh Street Berkeley, California 94710-1409

A CATALOG RECORD FOR THIS TITLE IS
AVAILABLE FROM THE LIBRARY OF CONGRESS

for my family

TABLE OF CONTENTS

My First Time

The boy wasn't painfully ugly. Sure, he had the normal teenage pockets of acne, but they didn't usurp his heart-shaped face. Rather, they flushed along his cheeks and hid near his earlobes, like little angry villages unable to mount an insurrection. And though a greasy, short-cropped cluster of hair resisted whatever combing he gave it, it wasn't totally without manners. His blue t-shirt was frayed on the right sleeve. I think he had blue eyes.

He must have seen the letters I toiled over during World History with Mr. Eddins, a name I associate not with a face but with the worn-away crotch of his jeans. I remember the letter written when Jeremy Fradin, the class clown, fell asleep. His snore alerted everyone and when Mr. Eddins slapped his desk to wake him, drool splashed up. When Lisa Barber refused to pledge allegiance and Mr. Eddins erupted and told her that she *damn well better show America some respect because those crazy kamikaze Japs killed my best friends*, I wrote the obvious jokes about the redirection of old Mr. Eddins's blood flow instead of mulling over the atrocities of epithets and wars. I cared less about condemning the letter's subject than I did about amusing the letters' recipient, Jaime, into falling wildly in love with me.

After all, Jaime was dangerous: two weeks into our friendship, he carved into his arm the name of a girl who wouldn't talk to him. *Kim* blazed on his arm, angry and pleading, for three weeks. I may have fallen in love with him then. He was *awkward genius*. I was *gossip storehouse*. Due to my dual roles as yearbook staff member and confidante to the senior cheerleaders, I knew that Brian was two-timing Angela a week before Angela flung his books out a school bus window, that Nicole was pregnant and by whom, that Jane, whose mother taught Modern Languages, got high every fourth period in the faculty parking lot. I knew, and I never said anything.

Everyone knew Jaime. He was definitely going to be the valedictorian, he was definitely going to Harvard, and he was *definitely* going to lord his Nobel Prize over the rest of us at reunions. It wasn't just the students who knew this; teachers also seemed dumbstruck by Jaime's intelligence. So he didn't get in trouble when he pissed on a desk in Miss Kushner's (empty) class, nor did he even get a slap on the wrist when he heaved a desk down a hallway. And when he wrote for Ms. Fritz's Honors English class an essay about the joys of punching German women who stifle his creativity, he was suspended for only three days.

I called the first time to find out what he had really written in that essay for English class; he told me instead about the time in fourth grade when he laid his dick on the projection machine "just to see what it would look like, enlarged." I was sixteen, overweight, miserably, effeminately gay: I tried to forget I had a penis every second of the day. So when, by the end of the year, Mr. Eddins was mixing up our names, I was blissful. I practiced combining my first name with his last name on notebook paper. I encoded symbols of my affection on modern-day papyrus while we studied ancient Egypt, I imagined him in togas during the Hellenistic period, and during the Inquisition I admitted to no one that I was in love with the resident genius freak of Western High.

I slipped notes into his hand as we passed—him going from English to History, me the other way around. I didn't miss a day.

And neither must've the greasy-haired boy. Every day he monitored the traffic of a love note between two guys. I had never noticed him before, but backgrounds and foregrounds blurred around Jaime: motions slowed to the speed of sunsets. As he took the note, Jaime's hand held mine briefly.

Unwittingly I had told my name to the boy dozens of times, each time louder, until my name thundered in him. And one day, I turned from Jaime's back to find him in front of me. He wasn't ugly; he was smiling, he was smaller than me by about four inches, he was so close he was going to kiss me. But then his hands shot to my shoulders, his lips opened, and he shoved "faggot" onto me. Spittle served as a glue to make the name stick.

I felt the cuts all over my body where the word made invisible grooves, where the label was already being sutured to my skin. He had friends behind him; behind me was an air-space made emptier by silent onlookers. Jaime was already in class, raising his brilliant hand to answer Mr. Eddins's questions. My hands were raising too; I shoved the boy as he walked away, smiling at his friends. I screamed after him, "Who's the faggot now?" But I had let too much time elapse. The name absorbed me.

I had called myself that name for as many days as I had known Jaime. I had waited until my own house was empty and stood in front of my mother's mirror and had said the words, "You are a faggot," and I had watched myself say it, falling to the cold tile of the bathroom floor, hugging my knees to my chest, waiting for something to happen. So, when it came swirling down upon me, it felt as if the name assaulted my hair, my chest, my legs from the outside, until it could find some vulnerable part of me, some place where the acidic spittle could melt through to the wellspring of *faggot* inside me. Then the dam broke and I was saturated with the name.

The Ends of Terror

1. Surrender

We've been refused at the doors of Southern Nights, the Blue Cactus, and a handful of other bars. But at the Parliament House, no one asks for ID. I'm nineteen, but look younger, thanks to a ball cap and baby face. There's no line to get in; the Parliament House has neither a bouncer nor an age restriction, but it does provide free lubricant and condoms in large, strategically placed baskets. Everywhere I look, men in various stages of undress throng the outside hallways of the club, a Motel 8 in its former life. There are two floors to the U-shaped building, perhaps two hundred rooms total. In its other incarnation, it catered to the Disney weekend tourist crowd. Now, guys who look even younger than me are chatting with bare-chested silver foxes. People above us are leaning over the railings, scoping the horde below. Men swarm the stairs. I can't move at all without feeling the friction of someone else's torso or back. I'm polite through the crowd, saying, "Excuse me," or "Sorry, man," to men who look annoyed at any hint of etiquette. The Parliament House is the closest thing to the French Quarter that I've ever seen. There's no music; the din of conversation manages to both cover and amplify the sexual tension. Johnny says, lighting a cigarette, "This is the real Magic Kingdom, kid."

And I do feel like a kid, naively overdressed in jeans and a t-shirt, not to mention the unsexy and wholly inaccessible briefs I have on underneath. It's a Saturday night in January, but winter means almost nothing in Florida. People blur by in hardly any clothing at all, or else they lie inside the rooms, naked on top of floral bedspreads, the door slung open, privacy gone nostalgic. In the outdoor halls of this hotel-cum-nightclub on Orange Blossom Trail, in the thundering heart of Orlando's red-light district, men touch without fear.

My friends prod me forward along the corridor. Steve and Johnny are both 26 and confident beyond their years. They've brought me to my first gay club, a fact they'd kept repeating in the car as they grinned at each other, as if they were about to hand over a decoder ring and my first copy of *The Gay Agenda*. Johnny and Steve scout from room to room. When their bodies jostle another man's, they just smile and jut their chins forward and say, "What's up?" Johnny's favorite pickup line is "Hey," and he says it every time he makes eye contact. He draws out the vowel, shading the word seductive.

But we are silent as church folk when we join the men watching outside uncurtained windows. The spectacle I find there shocks me: men having sex, making live scenes of the videos I keep at the bottom of a footlocker in my college dorm room. Men roll onto their stomachs, turning their faces toward the audience. We watch men tied to bedposts, their mouths agog, wincing from the stroke of the whip. Men on all fours, heads bowed. Hairy men shaved down, the body corrected. Blond men and brown-haired men, bald men, men of every ethnicity. Kneeling down, snaking their heads from all angles. Men holding other men by the jaw, pinching the nose closed so the mouth will open. Men lurching into other men, men receiving them. This is power: each man giving in, burning off his shame as he surrenders to another man's fantasy.

I nudge Steve and when he doesn't respond I swipe my elbow into his gut. He responds by pinching my nipple really, really hard. I look up to discover that Steve has sprouted a full beard, traded in his size-too-small jeans for leather chaps, and replaced the twinkle in his eye with a snarl. The stranger winks at me. I turn my head and lower my eyes. I raise them.

*

Later, I stand alone on the second level, facing away from the moans spilling out and down into the parking lot. Every kind of car glitters under the same moonlight. I am alone in an open-atrium whorehouse, overweight, out of place. Steve and Johnny have transformed themselves from longing onlookers into devoured actors; I think I saw Johnny's jockstrap in some rippling line-up of torso before someone closed the blinds in 213. *This* is the gay Shangri-La I've been pining for? The reality doesn't match the brochure.

A police officer strides from behind one of the building's brick wings. His motorcycle helmet, a polished white dome, gleams. The blue uniform stretches over a thick muscled body; his trousers are tucked neatly into leather boots. He has on oversized, mirrored sunglasses and a thick handlebar mustache. His badge will surely shine cleansing light into this sex prison; he will establish order in the chaos of desire.

The cop keeps walking, his hand raised to his chest, gripping a cord that streams backward over his left shoulder. The cord occasionally goes slack before he tugs it taut again. I watch his arm and chest flex. I imagine someone's car stuck in the mud or a fallen tree blocking the only exit. The cord is attached to an obstacle, but he's winning, he's moving forward. And then what is attached at the end of the cord emerges.

It's a man. Handcuffed. Attached to a leash. The leash hooks to a collar that extends into a leather hood covering the man's entire face. He can't see or feel his way. I don't even think he has shoes. He's naked except for a leather thong and a silver chain that runs between his nipples. Under the mask, forced night of no stars, he could be terrified or turned on, aghast and desperate for breath. He has willingly given over control of his body to another, a demigod in fetish gear, so that he may be free.

*

I don't remember leaving—or even much of what happened after I see the slave and his sergeant at different ends of the tether. I remember feeling hopeful and terrified at the cop's presence, before I knew he was only doing a cameo in his discipline-drag. I remember being seized by the thought: *We're going to jail.*

Part of me is still waiting for someone to place his hand squarely on my shoulder, tuck my head into a squad car, push me towards a badly made bed in some dimly lit cell, kicking my legs apart. Then I'll ask his name, and in the shadows of what we're supposed to say, what we're supposed to do, he won't answer. He'll slam shut the cell door, remaining on the inside, turning towards me with unzipped eyes.

2. Discipline and Punish

My brother Dustin sits in his car, listening to some eighties retro station while he waits for the line of vehicles to move from the surface street onto the Florida Turnpike. It's rush-hour traffic in Miami. Cars are backed up three lights. In the afternoon heat, Dustin sees a shirtless man jogging east, the smooth musculature of him glistening, backlit by the sunset. When the man is roughly parallel to Dustin's car, he stops to tie his shoe. That's when Dustin asks him if he wants a blowjob.

The man snaps up, his spine registering shock. His face contorts as he replays the question. He drops his hand to his crotch, roughly grabs himself, and says, "How about I shove this up your ass instead?" His penis is his weapon, alien to any economy of pleasure.

Dustin doesn't miss a beat when he says, "You have to buy me dinner first."

*

The man my brother propositions calls him later on his cell phone. His voice is a mixture of nervousness and business, a copper wire pulled tight. He asks for Dustin by name. He says where they met. He is matter-of-fact, a machine. Then he identifies himself as an agent in the FBI's bioterrorism unit; he took down Dustin's license plate number, fed it into some computer, and retrieved every phone number associated with the car. This man, this agent of the government invested with the public trust, imbued with the power to protect people, tells my brother that he and his FBI friends know where he lives and they are coming to kick his faggoty ass. He hangs up on my brother's sputtering apology.

Later that night he calls back. He has spoken with his superiors. The next day, at 1100 hours, Dustin will report to the Hialeah branch of the Federal Bureau of Investigation where he will be read his rights, fingerprinted, and questioned. Afterwards, he will be held until the FBI is satisfied that my brother is not at the heart of some gay-mafia plot to kill President Bill Clinton and, perhaps, redecorate the White House in shades of mauve. Dustin calls me with updates each time, until he finally arrives home. He is almost shaking, telling me every detail as we sit on my bed. I try to listen but all I want is to erase this from happening. I call the Miami office of the FBI, and the receptionist verifies that indeed the government employs this agent. When I hang up, Dustin knows the news isn't good.

"They're going to torture me."

"They're not going to torture you, Dustin."

"They're going to torture me."

My brother, the terrorist, has never been so sure of anything in twenty-two years of virginal life.

Imagine you've propositioned someone. Imagine they're attractive. You're attractive. Imagine you haven't done it in the nicest way possible: *hey, would you like a blowjob?* Not *how about a date, hot stuff?* Not *you have the best abs in all of Hialeah.* You believe, after all, that men cut to the chase. Honesty is rewarded. But most of all, when you see a muscle-cub with front-spiked hair running alongside a busy street in short red shorts you believe you're hitting on someone who'd be attracted to you. You haven't, for all of your twenty-two years, discerned the difference between the hypermasculine hetero army-type and the hypermasculine gay gym-rat. They are the same book you read the same way: with one hand.

After the FBI scheduled the interrogation, after the agent described how he and his friends were going to beat him bloody, after he'd harassed my brother for hours, Dustin finally told our parents.

Imagine you've already told your parents that you, a man, desire men. Imagine they didn't handle it well—your mother retreating so far into depression that she became a risk to your safety. You've gone through the years of therapy and emerged on the other side happy, part of a family who still lives together and operates a family business.

Now imagine you must tell your mother that a few hours ago you propositioned a stranger, repeating the words, "Do you want a blowjob," to your father, the man who thought that your friends had brainwashed you gay. Now tell your parents you are a matter of national security.

*

When the agent called to harass Dustin again, my father answered. We listened on speakerphone in the next room, hitting the button that muted our line. The conversation was over quickly. My father never lost his cool. He allayed each of the agent's fears. Straight guy to straight guy. He painted a picture.

Imagine you're with your buddies, he started. *Yeah.* It's Friday, end of a long week, you want to blow off some steam. *With you so far.* Imagine some pretty girl in a short skirt walks by, you say something stupid. Now you wouldn't normally say something like that, would you? *Um.* Would you? *Sorry for taking up your time, Mr. Hall. Consider the matter closed.*

3. Psychotic Gods

"I want to shit on your chest," the man I'm having phone sex with says. His voice had grown coarser in the fifteen minutes we'd been talking. When he asked me if I was into anything freaky, I guess I probably should have said no but his voice, an equal blend of animal lust and stark precision, deep and rumbling, persuaded me. When he wanted to shave me, fine. I fetched my electric razor and shaved down patches of my already smooth thigh. When he wanted to spank me I put the phone down on the bed so he could hear me hit my palm. No way was I going to beat my ass red for some freak on the phone.

Now, however, he wants to use me as some combination of commode and serving platter. He wants to do the grossest thing I've ever heard.

When I was a kid, my parents kept a bookshelf stocked with inappropriate books. Among the Steven King titles were books dealing with occult rituals and healing, a series of Harlequin Romances that I devoured by age nine, and a biography of Hitler called *The Psychopathic God*. That title, gold-threaded on red binding, begged to be read. I remember, really, only the very lurid details: Hitler had one testicle. Hitler fancied himself an artist. Hitler liked to defecate on Eva Braun.

I ask the man on the phone how many testicles he has. His voice turns cobalt. "Two," he says, sternly. First the air, then the line that tethers us goes slack.

*

That year I couldn't stand to have a man touch my body, to put his hand on my chest, to put two fingers down my waistband, to graze his lips on my neck—that year I had sex with men's voices. Nights, I existed in a kind of virtual Parliament House, a phone party line where I could remake myself into whatever I pleased.

I like to think I was a good sport—if I wasn't exactly into what got the other guy off, I'd try to carry it out as much as I possibly could without laughing. Once, I was talking to a guy in Saudi Arabia. We'd exchanged all the normal things: false names and stats, foreplay and body contact, oral sex and lots of kissing, which really amounted to a lot of slobbering of the mouth on the receiver. That always turned me off; it sounded like someone had put his mouth over your entire ear and was swabbing the deck inside. But when he said he wanted to pour Coke on my ass and lick it off, I broke. I laughed until the tears welled up. I'd barely caught my breath before I realized he'd hung up.

Mostly, I tried to respect them, even if I couldn't exactly imagine a life with these men and their fetishes, their bi-curiosities, their wives. Even when they wanted pretty gross stuff, I tried to believe that what is found in language is found in nature. Men who wanted every part of themselves worshipped. Men who demanded I answer the phone, "I'm ready for you sir," then proceeded to fantasize about my bound wrists, my blindfolded face. I said back "Please," allowing the edge in my voice to sharpen. I said it to understand my self-debasement, my loathing for what returned my stare in the mirror. In their want was tactility, a love. We were each inventing something on the other end. Maybe they only wanted a voice to stave off the loneliness. But me? I wanted to be degraded. I wanted to pick from ruin the parts that remained whole.

4. The Pleasurable Is Political

She is smiling when she says, "Rape isn't about sex, it's about power. That's why it's hot." She takes out a cigarette from the pack beside her on the log. One of the men produces a lighter, and her hand holds his firmly, a little too long, steadying the flame. The woman—a writer who will, a year later, extol the virtues of anal sex while buying my friend and me drinks—is surrounded by her students, her voice both luscious and too loud among the bullfrogs' croaking. The boys are laughing as she blows smoke rings. Her mouth overexaggerates.

We are supposed to be inside the converted carriage barn, listening to a poet read his latest work about desire. But the Vermont summer night is uncannily cool, and so we sit outside to be entertained by a woman whose lipstick matches her orange cotton blouse. I am the only man not caught up in her raspy cobra laugh. I am not like the other men, breathing in her heady perfume mixed with sweat, the day's fragrant wear on the body. They look at each other conspiratorially. I imagine each one's penis stiffening under blue denim, then their bodies in the lake behind us, pale shoulders rising up out of the water, the woman watching from her log. My laugh joins the fray.

*

"I try to avoid fraternity row," my friend Tracy says as we take a detour toward town on our way to campus. We are seniors at Stetson University, both majoring in English. Tracy is six-foot-four and weighs about four hundred pounds. She's stuffed into her side of the beat-up truck. Her arms are tattooed with daggered hearts and half-naked nymphs. Tracy is the first lesbian I know who insists on being called a "bull dagger." I like Tracy, even if she does sport the greasiest mullet I've ever seen. I do not, however, like either of her two girlfriends, the "baby butches" whose names I can't ever get right. Tracy is, she explains, "man enough for two women."

I ask her why she avoids the tiny street flanked on either side by fraternity houses. It would save fifteen minutes and we're almost late to class. She looks at me, reaches behind my seat, and brings out a sawed-off shotgun. It's loaded, she says, and my question changes. She has sharp cheekbones that make her eyes seem far away, small. When I ask her why she keeps a loaded gun in her car, her eyes narrow further. Her knuckles whiten on the wheel. "There's only so many times you can hear 'Let's rape a dyke!' before you start to carry insurance."

*

What if we all went traitor to penetrative sex? Left that country for good. Your hand caressing my face, my hand on yours. How would I recognize you? How would you terrorize me then?

*

A few months into our relationship, I let Brandon tie me up. He binds my wrists with silk ties to his headboard. "You're my prisoner," he growls playfully, rubbing two days worth of stubble over my chest. Soon after he penetrates me, my wrists begin to throb. I don't say anything. I locate the dull pain, the pleasure of its throb. Brandon is so clearly enjoying this play, I can't stop it.

Sex hurts. My stomach twists itself into knots with the quick jabs inside me, but I grit my teeth. After a while, I discover a place inside of pain that feels almost-good, just when the momentum stills—he's not pushing forward or drawing out, there is no torque. It's the place inside pain where the membrane is thinnest, where the searing quality threatens to hurt you, but then you feel it lessen, release its hold. That's where people like me live during intercourse.

That night, after he unties me, kisses me, leaps up to shower, I roll over on the bed, rub my wrists right. Later, holding me against him in the bed, Brandon tells me that he loves me. I pretend to be asleep. I'm crying in the dark.

5. Sex Trial: A Fantasy

I want so much from violence: thesis and antithesis, to make the orgasm a reward for hard work, as if it proves I am a red-blooded American man, operating inside the matrix of the Puritan theory of pleasure. I want testimony to the fact I've suffered—and in the face of it, survived. I want a sweat-stained record admitted into evidence, exhibit ménage à trois. What would be more pleasurable than denying violence its power?

I want pleasure to sweep into the courtroom wearing a black veil, Joan Collins-style, a surprise last witness, allowed despite the slick defense attorney's objections. Pleasure cannot be overruled. I want sensual delight to swear it will tell the truth this time. I want desire to coo, "Hello, lover," at my jailer and then undress, button after button nimbly undone, until all artifice is left in well-tailored pieces on the floor. Let the judge dismiss all charges.

I am home from college for winter break, my second year of school. I haven't told my parents I'm gay yet. I am working up the courage. I've been to the Parliament House twice now, though I've never done more than watch with silent judgment. I have perfected the art of disdaining what I want. I have come out to friends; I have been elected president of the queer student organization. I have not kissed a man. I am paralyzed by desire. Soon, I'll find a number for gay phone entertainment in the back of my straight older brother's *Rolling Stone* magazine.

It's two in the morning and I am wide awake, staring at my reflection in the bathroom mirror. Earlier that day I slipped into my mother's bathroom to steal her rouge, her shimmering eye shadow, a rainbow of lipsticks. I secreted away two sponges, lip liner, fake eyelashes, her nail polish. I planned to change my form.

I work in the moonlight refracted by the frosted window. In that confessional, I paint my face. I dab the foundation into the palm of my hand. I use a wedge-shaped sponge to dash it across my forehead, sweeping down my cheeks, across my jawline, down where the neck dovetails into collarbone. I rub with two fingers so there'll be no lines, no witness to corroborate my falsehood. I powder. I brush my cheeks with rouge, affix lashes. I pad my eyelids with gold shimmer, massage traces of the eye shadow into my cheeks. I line my lips, making them fuller by drawing another mouth, a mute twin, a half centimeter above. I spread across my lips a blue-red veneer. Lune Rousse, my mother's lipstick—it queens me otherworldly, Russian moonscape, luminous ruse, lunatic roused from slumber.

In the mirror I am not beautiful.

Some other metallic face looks back, alien. Then I'm wracked with nerves, a strange form of guilt. What if my brother, or, worse—my mother—discovers flecks of makeup on the bathroom rug, on the counter? What if my new face never washes off, what if I glitter forever? I raise the camera I've brought with me. I snap the picture.

*

Once, coming home from a night out with Tracy and our friends Robin, Trish, and Robyn (the self-termed bull dyke quartet), I notice some disturbance to my door. I can see where something has trickled downwards, though the liquid has already dried. Small traces of white foam have hardened in tiny vertical rivulets. When I get closer, I see a word spelled out on my door in what must have been shaving cream. Someone has sprayed the letters "FAGG" on my grimy dorm room door. But shaving cream is an unstable medium; it has emulsified and then evaporated. The misspelled word is only visible because it cleaned the door, leaving a shine, readable because it erased the dirt.

That night, I stay up until dawn, cutting up various newspapers I've grabbed on the way out of the clubs I frequent, making a collage of images. Women in tuxedos dipping each other in a ballroom. Women kissing women in the Stock Exchange. Drag queens in their splendor, surrounded by applauding crowds. Images of RuPaul, of George Michael and Melissa Etheridge and Elton John and Shakespeare. Selected quotes that trumpet the slogan "Proud to Be Gay." At six thirty in the morning, I staple the collage to the corkboard outside my door. I let "FAGG" blaze on. I sleep soundly.

By evening, the corkboard has been ransacked, the drag queens shredded, and on the cement-block wall someone has posted a sign comprised of two stick figures, one of whom bends at the waist as the other fucks him from behind. The sign reads "A.I.D.E.S KILLS FAGGS DEAD." I grab a pen from my satchel. I correct the wrong words.

*

The photograph never comes out. It stays a bruise-dark blur, refusing shape and color. I am relieved and terrified that I will live this way forever.

PROPHECY

There is no telling what I am, what I'll do, so I lift the lighter to my hair. The thumb-sized flame crackles as it meets the hard ridge of my Aqua-Netted, Morrissey-inspired pompadour. My audience laughs, four boys like me who have endured the first week of college orientation, their faces smiling each beneath baseball caps. The odor of singed hair fills the room. I would burn my head bald for them. I would singe every hair on my body to kiss Jamie, a constantly grinning boy who lays on his stomach on the bottom bunk of his bed, his pale face propped up by his hands, enthralled as my hair dissolves into smoke. He's the one who has kidded me into doing this, into making my hair an effigy. "Dude," he'd said, grinning at me the way boys do when they want to dare you, "your hair is so gay."

Tony, a skinny twin who can't dance and is thus always dancing, sprays the Aqua-Net into the lighter's flame. My head ignites, an orange periphery surrounding me, and the laughter is harder to hear beyond the quick ball of fire. Jamie rushes a recently used shower towel over my head, and I am dampened, smoldering, laughing, even though I know my hair, my pride, is a disaster. I feel the fire scorching down into the soft part of me, where I hate myself. Self-immolating fool, clown who tries to make boys love me—boys who would, without doubt, feel betrayed if they discovered the truth about what I am.

That night, I dream Jamie's face closer to mine, our heads making a tent underneath the wet blue cloth. He says, "I want to fire you."

That year, at frat parties where guys unzip and wave their dicks around, at the urinals in the Student Union bathroom, in the showers where my dorm-mates pass out drunk in their underwear while the water streams down and over their bodies, at times in the common rooms where jocks lounge in shorts that ride up when a leg is thrown over the arm of a lucky chair, I avert my eyes. I live in a double-occupancy room in Gordis Hall, on a Baptist campus, in the small town in which I grew up but left. I live a returned townie life. I live it in fear. If I don't keep the flame of me buried, it will engulf me, send a signal into the dark, dissolve me into so much putrid smoke. What I am should be extinguished.

*

We know the morality of characters in fairy tales by their hair. "Golden sunshine in her hair," Merryweather opines, blessing the infant Princess Aurora before she is cursed to sleep. The same words fall from Maleficent's mouth, but twist into curse, as if she is pleased that all that sunshine will go to waste, as if by rendering the maiden unconscious the land itself is cured of moral righteousness.

Think of the Little Mermaid, the sacrifices that were made for her form. Her devoted sisters, having heard through the underwater grapevine that Ariel forever forfeited her fins because her beloved wed another, offer their own hair to the Sea Witch. In exchange, the hag gives them a knife that Ariel must use to kill the Prince in order to regain her mermaid figure. Of course, her heart breaks at the sight of her shorn sisters, their bald heads bobbing like jellyfish in the open blue water. But she cannot bring herself to kill; her sisters' hair has taught her nothing if not self-sacrifice.

Think of Rapunzel, letting that stud traipse up her trellis. Think of the hero, lost in the glorious folds of her hair, exalting in the thick ropes of what he must come to think of as Rapunzel's most private self. So that when the witch, with her over-processed perm and wretched split ends, divests Rapunzel of her hair, the hero has no clue he is climbing into the clutches of evil.

Hair bewitches men. It is the currency of desire, the prophecy I listen to.

*

Once, I dyed my hair red, let the front grow out long until the thick strand reached the nape of my neck. Little flame, unfurling in the wind. I wanted hair I could let down.

Once, I car-flirted my way down to Key West with a man who sped up and smiled. The hair flew over my face, out the window, toward him. My hair, a bridge that beckoned, a line not strong enough to cross.

Once, I watched two South American men play tennis on the courts outside a friend's apartment. They played poorly while I smoked. My lipstick left my Marlboros red-kissed. One of the men hit the ball over the fence, and it bounced onto the concrete and landed on the second-floor level, where I caught it. The players stopped. I held the ball out, Eve proffering an apple. The retriever came loping up the steps, the more athletic one with short hair and a liquid smile. I made one up when he asked my name. I asked if he wanted a drink, and he waited there on the terrace. He drank the water while looking into my eyes. The sweat made his skin shine through his shirt. I wanted more when the cup was empty.

Once there was no artifice, only a real body, a hand touching it, saying, *You are my beloved, and that is how I know I am real.* But that was just a fairy tale: no body is real.

I tried giving up desire. The prayer would start, *Please let me wake up different.*

Once, I was a man below, a woman on top, a palimpsest that made me less clear to the world and made the world clearer to me.

Once I was not a satyr, a eunuch; not trans- or bi- or uni-.

Not prefixed.

Once I was afraid my roots were showing. Then, I was afraid that no one would see them.

Hours spent standing behind my mother, her hair unwashed and knotted, a cigarette smoldering down to its filter in the ashtray beside her chair. Hours taking the brush through the matted blond mess, my mother saying, "Brush it harder," telling me how when she was a child her brother used to drag her through the yard, caveman-style, by her hair. I grew up in front of the television. Behind my mother's head, I watched Merv Griffin, Sally Jesse, reruns of *Green Acres*. I loved how the comb organized the hair, then reorganized it, again and again. My middle-parted, side-parted, zigzag-parted mother; feathered mother; faux-beehived mother; diagonal mother; mother waiting to be French-braided, pigtailed, side-ponied, a woman waiting to be made or unmade by my hands.

*

My boyfriend overhears an older white woman say to his co-worker Yoli, "Why do you and that other woman have such different hair?"

Yoli is East African and wears her hair natural, while Charlotte, the coworker to whom the white lady gestures, has her hair locked into long dreads. Yoli, Charlotte, and Brandon work in a discount bookstore in Rice Village, in Houston, a semi-posh sixteen-block outdoor shopping center. For Brandon and Charlotte, time slows.

"Maybe because we're two fucking different people," Yoli snaps.

The manager reprimands her, says, "For Chrissakes, Yoli, it's only hair!"

He demands she apologize. She does. Then he fires her.

*

When I was a kid, my grandmother's chief responsibility in life was to visit her sick elderly friends and gift them the potted, unflowering plants that she grew in her greenhouse. She was visiting one such a friend, a half-hearing woman whose muumuu looked plastic. My younger brother Dustin and I played hide-and-seek in the large dark house, crawling behind couches, hiding on the enclosed porch. When it was time to go, grandma's friend remarked how nice it was to meet Janey and Dotty. Afterward, in the heavy car ride silence, I saw in my grandmother's tight-drawn mouth a plan forming.

My first haircut took place in a barbershop, complete with a Marvy barber pole and townsmen reading the paper, my grandmother standing by, her pocketbook cradled in the crook of her arm. The barber was rough. He'd grab a length of hair, pull it taut between two callused fingers, snip. His belly pressed against the back of my head while he cut. "These boys look… different," he said to my grandmother, who sent him an imploring look: yes, change them.

"Different" meant I looked like a little girl. A few weeks earlier at the park where my older brother played soccer, a man asked to photograph me on the monkey bars. I was flattered. He told me, "Ask your mommy first," which I did. My mother met the man, and then retreated back to my brother's soccer game. I posed on the bars, on the ground, smiling for the man, his quickening shutter finger. At the end of our session he stroked my hair and said, "You are such a pretty little girl." Inside, my heart quivered: *I was pretty* was true if *I was a girl* was true.

My scalp throbbed under the barber's hands, his flat black comb, which he pulled out of his cutter's belt, where he kept scissors and razors and other instruments of torture. My hair was cut across my forehead, lifted above my ears, nearly flat in the back and on the sides. After he was done my grandmother stooped to the ground, collecting a handful of hair she deposited in one of those opaque plastic envelopes she'd brought for the occasion. She paid the man but did not tip him. She took us for ice cream. Sitting on a picnic bench along the town's main drag, my grandmother beamed at the passersby. She ate her sugar cone expertly, saying more than once, "I'm so glad to be out on a date with my handsome young *men*." We were her courtiers, minted heterosexuals, out for granny delights.

"What the fuck did you do to my kids," my mother said upon sight of us.

"Now, Marsha. Just gave them haircuts. It's what grandmothers do." She sniffled. "They needed it."

"They needed it" was my grandmother's motto, what she said after we unwrapped socks on Christmas, or after she'd refolded all the towels in my mother's bathroom closet on the nights she babysat. "They needed it" was also what my mother called fightin' words.

My mother hugged us to her body; we were little human shields in the yelling that passed over their bodies. It ended when my grandmother slammed out and my father opened the door and said to her retreating form,

"This is how you slam a door." It rattled the windows.

*

My grandmother permed her hair every two weeks at the beauty school where she paid ten dollars and asked the woman to please clean out her ears. She was devoid of shame. And she let me waste reams of paper at her typewriter on rainy afternoons. I'd sit at the card table and hammer the keys just to hear the language strike home. Nothing was more satisfying than the zing and swoosh of the carriage return or the miracle of replacing corrective tape. Only at her typewriter did I want to be a mechanic, to understand metal parts moving in concert. She gave me Harlequin Romance novels to read for inspiration. Genuine bodice-rippers, with covers depicting cotton-bosomed women swept into some Fabio's embrace.

Once, after loving one of those novels so much, I typed a fan letter to the author. My grandmother wrote the cover letter, explaining my young age, saying how I'd spend hours at her typewriter. "Budding writer," she called me, and if she had said the words aloud, I think her voice would have had an air of pride about it.

*

My mother's father had a full head of hair when he died in 1995, the summer after my freshman year of college. He was 68, living alone in one of those comfortable houses on a tree-shaded street in Orange City, a few towns over from where I went to school. He called where he lived Sun City, erasing the gap between the two words. My mother hadn't talked to her father in years before he went into the Volusia County Hospital. But I had.

My roommate Sean and I used to prank call my mother's father. It started innocently enough, with Sean phoning as a lost pizza-delivery man. My grandfather, always polite to strangers, thought he was delivering to a neighbor: "If you pass Mano's, well now you've gone too far," he advised. When Sean repeated the address, Pa sputtered out, "But well that's my house!" Sean concluded, "Old man, you are paying for this pizza."

If Pa was proud of one thing, it was his virility. As a senior citizen, he'd had two seventeen-year-old girlfriends and had been arrested for soliciting sex from an undercover police officer in a park. (A male officer, at that.) My grandfather was nothing if not a man of vim and vigor. And so Sean's off-the-cuff taunt got Pa steaming mad. He informed Sean that he wasn't paying "for no pizza from a little pussy." Sean got quiet, his face gaining its Irish blush. "You're paying for this pizza, asshole, or I'm going to kill you." I muffled my guffaws with a pillow.

Pa screamed into the phone, "Bring it on! Bring it on, pizza man!" We could hear someone—a woman—in the background saying, "Clayton, honey, who *is* it?" It was either Mentora, the woman he was seeing before my grandmother's funeral, or Anne, who my aunts told me worshipped Satan, which meant she was probably Presbyterian.

After that first prank call, my grandfather opened his front door to a dazzling array of pizza boxes strewn over his lawn. My dorm-mates called him weekly, hollering into the receiver, "Bring it *on!*"

Two things surprised me: one, that he never called the cops. The other was that my grandfather kept his hair throughout this ordeal. "He looks like Hitler," my cousin Shanda said, looking down into the coffin at his funeral. His head was propped up on a pillow, as if he were just about to lurch out of the box. He *did* look like Hitler—he had a thin mustache at the time of his death and his hair was cut short and swept from the left side to the right. His forehead was pale and shiny, his hair dark and oily. But I don't know if Shanda would have said that if the stories about him hadn't been handed down, circulated now among the grandkids.

Shanda kept cracking jokes and my cousin Travis kept laughing. I smirked my allegiance to their irreverence but somehow my eyes kept wandering over to the dirty old man in the box. I kept thinking, I will inherit that receding hairline, I will inherit that head, the way the eyes sink back into the skull. I wanted to hear the dead man ask: what other parts of me would you like?

*

I never saw my father cut his hair in my life. He never went to a barber, a salon. He cut it himself, with an electric razor. His hair was fine, black, and wavy. In pictures of a younger self, my dad was always clean-cut, shaved beneath controlled locks of hair that he parted on the side. Though I have my mother's straight hair, it's my father's hairstyle I emulated for so long, brushed straight over to one side, forthright.

In a picture of my dad reading the newspaper, I am reading over his shoulder, hunched down next to him, nearly cheek-to-cheek. It's a posed photograph, I think for a high school journalism assignment. My dad is wearing a green shirt, and I'm dressed for school in a red Roman-collared shirt, my hands tucked into my jeans. What is striking about the photograph is not the age of the people in it, nor the fact that I am seemingly interested in the sports page. From the downward angle of the lens, my dad and I look like hair-twins, our parts smiling identically for the camera.

*

I keep moving between the past and the present, following one strand of time to the root of memory and back. I separate the layers of the past, braid us in the present tense.

*

Towards the end of his life, my father couldn't comb his hair. He used a special brush with an extended handle that angled the brush back and away. It was designed for people who can't lift their hands above their head, for people like my dad who had cardiac surgery.

Then he couldn't use even that.

Couldn't shave. Couldn't wash his own body. Cook his own meals. Brush his teeth. Then he had no more teeth to brush. Some days he couldn't remember how to stand.

After it was washed and combed, his hair sat smooth against his scalp, almost restoring him, nearly again the debonair and mischievous man my mother once fell in love with.

*

I drive to Harmar, Pennsylvania, to be changed.

The man is shaving my head in a hotel room that I have paid for. It has a Jacuzzi and a late checkout time. He brought electric clippers and a cache of blue Gillette razors, the disposable kind, which he opens with his teeth.

"Only real men have hair," he says. The cuttings fall in clumps down my face. I lick my lips and stalks of hair stick to my tongue.

I have given up my right to say when the sacrifice is enough. It is never enough.

My chest is next. He holds the razor to my lips. I look up at him, a twenty-something with the hard edge of nowhere in his eyes. "Go on," he says, and I do. Two blades, one laying over the other, a small gap between. I kiss the metal lips.

He slides the twin blades over my pectorals, over where I breathe and bleed. Then he shaves his name, three block letters, on my left thigh. My right leg goes completely. My groin.

I am hairless, powerless as Samson, raw as silk. "Now," he says, "kiss my hairy chest."

After it is over, giving in, giving over, his body sated, gone, I, who normally close my eyes to put on deodorant lest a glimpse of naked body be caught, gaze into the full-length mirror. I trace the flexed muscles of my smooth legs, my hairless chest, my soldier buzzcut. The stubble on my neck seems the hairiest part of me. What stares back from the mirror is ready for whatever comes next. I am stripped, vulnerable, ready.

In the car, driving home, I roll down the windows. I turn up the radio. I sing along to the anthems all the way home.

SUICIDE MEMORABILIA

People try to die. They try and try. You know a girl, a friend of your brother's, who tried to drown herself in the kitchen sink, her hand heavy on the back of her own head until she was soaked to the shoes. You know the girl who brought a gun to school and put it in her mouth and pulled the trigger in front of her Spanish class, but couldn't figure out how to take the safety off. You know the jokes people have made of these girls. You've made the jokes too, repeated them to friends. You never wondered what these girls were drowning under, what they were trying to kill in themselves.

When you see your mother with a gun, you think it's you.

*

My mother sits on an unmade queen-size bed, her left heel tucked underneath her so that a bare knee juts out from her body. White as marble, it girds her body and absorbs the violent shudders that pass. My mother can make her body shudder at will, so that she looks as if a round of earthquakes is assaulting her from underneath. Usually, she does it to say that the present situation has become untenable, that those present have caused her to retreat inside of herself, where the damage is volcanic.

No one can know this place—it is, perhaps, a performance that makes even my mother a part of the audience. A way of disengaging, of speaking without the mouth. Forcing the body to testify that harm has been done. The first time it happened I was away at college. My brother Dustin described it to me over the phone. There'd been a family fight, of the kind that exceeded decorum as much as it did the midnight hour. At three a.m., my mother had *had enough*. She went stone quiet, letting her cigarette burn itself out in the ashtray on her lap. The argument raged around her, with my father yelling at my brothers from where he sat in his bed, next to my mother, and my brothers yelling back from where they sat on the floor near the foot of the bed. My mother rose from the bed, dumping the full ashtray all over, and walked zombielike down the hall to my bedroom. There, she lay down on my bed and began to whisper-repeat one word, *hands*, over and over again. My father and brothers tried to stop the shaking, tried to make her warm. Dustin described her face as frozen in terror, her eyes wide, her hands locked at her side. She wouldn't say anything else for a long time, and when her eyes finally showed recognition, the argument was a distant memory.

We knew whose hands she was talking about. We knew that once, as a girl, my mother woke from sleep because she could not breathe, woke to her father's lips pressed on hers. The shaking always said, *Look what you're doing to me.* The shaking always meant, *Now you're molesting me.* She doesn't reserve this kind of catatonic-shaking behavior for private. No, my mother has done this in the cereal aisle at the grocery store, at the For Eyes Vision Center, at our favorite Mexican restaurant.

Now, however, my mother is alone in the room, the smaller of the two bedrooms of the apartment my brother and I are renting in Houston, where I have enrolled in a doctoral program. My father and mother have just moved in with us. Dustin and I share the master bedroom in an apartment that totals just over 1,100 square feet. My parents' bedroom is the smaller of the two, crowded by a small writing desk, a tall dresser, two slim bookshelves, and the bed. The bed is splayed out on the floor without benefit of frame or box spring.

Three lumpy pillows buffer my mother from the wall; the wall is sullied by the pillows, as if my mother's frame sprouts dull wings. The gun oscillates over her chest. It negates the vases full of fake purple flowers and cheaply framed photographs of my mother's mother, a woman we called Gran, whose smile gleams out from the bedside table, the bookshelf, the overcrowded computer desk, the nightstand which she shares only with the latest Sylvia Browne titles, books on communicating with the dead that are always called something like *Contacting Your Spiritual Guide* or *Past Lives and How to Change Them.* If my mother isn't reading up on the afterlife, she's wasting valuable Nielsen points on John Edwards's smarmy show, *Crossing Over.* My mother is the kind of woman who stays on hold for guest psychics on radio shows, asking about my grandmother, asking how she died.

The gun is, in fact, my grandmother's, a pearl-handled .22 that my mother swept up in her arms while my other aunts were arguing over jewelry after my grandmother died. The gun is currently resting under her sunny yellow sweatshirt, its mouth pressed at an angle against my mother's breast. The gun makes an outline like a crooked, accusatory finger in the sweatshirt. This is the gun I've seen my mother draw on herself, the gun I've seen taken from her over and over. My father is knocking at the door. My brother is watching outside the window. My mother is saying, "I just want to go and see my mom now."

Afterwards, my mother crumples into a sobbing mess. After the gun is taken away, my mother has no control. The quakes grow louder, they double her over, she fights for breath. My mother will not get rid of the gun. It has sentimental meaning. An heirloom, even if it isn't exactly the gun my grandmother used to killed herself.

*

"She always called, Larry. Things would get bad between her and Pa, but she'd call us kids and at least say goodbye." My mother's hushed voice barely reaches over Madonna's, straining for a high note on the radio. My mother doesn't want to draw attention to the conversation from me or my brothers, who are still arguing over who called the plush, wide back seat in the shiny black and silver van we've just recently purchased. I like to pretend the vehicle is not someone's cast-off secondhand clunker, but is instead a space-age rocket, equipped with swiveling chairs and a miniature icebox where Pepsi chills in blue-and-silver cans. I like its large size, its carpeted floorboard that camouflages my creeping toward the cockpit. I like to crouch behind my parents' seats, listen to them talk about the failing marriage of our next-door neighbors, the alcoholics whose younger child is my nemesis. I am on a fact-finding mission, eager for new weapons to use against him but instead I hear them talking about my grandmother's suicide.

I had never seen Gran angry, never heard her say a cross word to people. She was witty and smart, and, like most eccentric people, indulged others' oddities. She never, to my knowledge, got upset when her mother-in-law, Grandma Hawkins, stole her jewelry and wore it around town, proclaiming this opal trinket or that ruby brooch had been gifted her by an admiring beaux. I think Gran was amused by Grandma Hawkins's sticky fingers and her amusement only grew when she could flesh out Grandma Hawkins's stories to check-out clerks, bank tellers, and fast food cashiers around their small Indiana town. I can't reconcile my Gran—the woman who even at fifty was castrating her own bulls and feeding chickens and mowing the lawns, the woman who smoked until diagnosed with lung cancer, and not a day after that—with the one my mother is talking about, the woman who shot herself through the heart. "She didn't call us, Larry, she didn't tell a soul."

I hear other details too: Pa found her dead in the hospital bed she'd slept in, in the living room. Pa told people he was so distraught upon finding her that he ran outside and tore apart one of the bushes before placing a calm phone call to the police department. I hear that Pa has been having an affair with a woman named Mentora; that Gran's life insurance policy names him a small-fortune beneficiary; that Gran's glasses were off and folded on a table, and she never took those glasses off, not even to sleep; that Gran's temple was bruised purple, there were bruises around her wrists, that she had shot herself with the wrong hand.

No fingerprints were taken, no autopsy performed.

My mother keeps insisting, "I know he did it. He did it, or he hired someone to do it. She talked about killing herself, but she'd never actually do it. She'd call us up, us kids, and say goodbye." My father nods quietly, raising the volume a bit on the radio, emitting a soft "uh-huh" in agreement.

My mother shakes a cup filled with shaved ice into her mouth and grinds the chips down. As her jaw chews, a slight popping sound can be heard, a muscular music which accompanies her mind's reworking of the case. "Pa killed her. The bruises, the wrong hand, the money, and they had been arguing a lot lately. He did it. I know it." Just then, the radio becomes silent, the van comes out of the canopy of trees into open air and my mother's face is bathed in golden light, her blond hair made into a luminous crown.

I am ten years old. The most I know about violence comes from half-assed punches thrown at recess on the playground. Damage is more accidental than anything. My mother's words make a shimmering, terrible truth.

I am a meddlesome child learning to hate his grandfather.

It's early spring when we drive the three days to Indiana, arriving just after a late March snow has blanketed the ground. The Best Western in Brownstown does not live up to its name. The room has three dead cockroaches, a fact I beg to leave my head as I help unpack the van. In all, it takes five of us three trips to unload. We've packed for a week. During those three trips back and forth to the car, I notice someone has built a snowman in the center of the outdoor courtyard, near a defunct and icy fountain. The snowman's arms have fallen off, his head partially melted in the afternoon glow. It's a nice day, though more frigid than I've packed for. I'm cold and angry, and I keep praying to God, asking Him to please give my grandfather AIDS, so that he will suffer and die. When I catch myself, I wonder where the golden light is for me, and when it does not come, I know my allegiance belongs to something darker than knowledge. I am not too young to know the word *revenge*.

*

"I love your father," my mother says as we sit talking on the steps outside the apartment in Houston. She's smacking an unopened end of a silver-foiled pack of cigarettes against the gray concrete steps. I remember imitating this same motion with my own Marlboro Light 100s, hammering the thick paper package down so that the tobacco flakes retreat into their paper casing. I'm amazed by the memory: it isn't until I'm four months outside of nicotine withdrawals that I recognize in my mother a former version of myself. "I love your father," she repeats, singling out one of her menthols and then looking up at me. "But more like a brother."

I can't stop from shriveling my forehead, my mouth turns downward. "You know," my mother continues, "your father is awful in bed."

On the scale of things to never say to your children, this one scores off the charts. I wait for the men in silver suits to surround us, to tear off our clothes and spray us with radiation-removing solvent right then and there. No one comes. The day does not darken, clouds do not rush into the place where the wound has left a vacuum. A bluejay trills in the magnolia tree beside the open-aired stairwell. I open my mouth several times to start a sentence. "I…" and "Well…" and "So…" spark and sputter out of my mouth. My mother stubs her cigarette out on the step. Flakes of charred tobacco spring into the wind.

*

My father tells me about the men my mother loved *un*like a brother. Now that she has left again, this time for a man in Dallas, my father gives me the details I wish I did not want to know. But I do. I picture my mother with each of her men. I think of my mother in bed with them, finding the passion and sheer masculine beauty absent in my pudgy, dry-humored father. My mother belongs to the world of reckless romance novels, the world of cheeky and glamorous women whose lives were constantly redefined by the epiphany desire brings. These heroines wielded power that would know no bounds. I too wanted to be that necessary.

*

The married man who owned the condo next door to the one in Daytona Beach that my mother used to clean. The wife found out and called our house. Dustin, the baby of the family, had just turned two.

The doctor she met at a flea market. My father found his card in her jeans a few months later. Dustin had just turned six.

A married police officer she met in her capacity as a safety guard. His wife was another crossing guard, my mother's friend. Dustin was eleven, and I was twelve, when the affair started. I remember this man knocking on our door, I remember his police cruiser, its wide nose and black bra, which he parked very close to our front door, on the lawn. I remember living in a town of people who parked their cars on their lawns. But what I remember most about this towering man is his dark hair and handlebar mustache, his gruffness, his large hands on the door as I opened it for him. My mouth went dry at the angle he cut in the doorway.

The man she was living with in Jacksonville, for whom she left my father just before I moved to Houston. I called him Mr. Panties after finding out he likes to cross-dress. I know this is unkind and I don't give a damn.

*

One night in 2005, my brother and I were sitting on the couch in our apartment, talking about our parents again, trying to understand what it was we witnessed, what it was that we were made to carry. I recalled the time we were kids and our mother was getting ready to go out, how my father said, "Nice cans" to her, how she received it like a terminal diagnosis. Dustin remembered cleaning their bedroom when we were teenagers, finding love letters the cop had sent. "I remember exclaiming, 'Good for her,' when you showed them to me," I said. We both laugh a little to mask the sadness.

Dustin had yet to experience a relationship with a man. Even though he basically lived at the gym and his biceps were as big as baby seals; even though he inherited the dark long lashes and glamorous good looks of my mother's line; even though he dressed as impeccably as any gay man I know; even though he had lots of friends, my brother hadn't sustained a romantic relationship past the two-month mark. He couldn't help the distrust welling up in him whenever he dated a man.

Dustin ended our conversation with a sigh. "I'm tired of thinking, whenever a man tells me 'I love you,'—I'm tired of looking back at him and thinking to myself, 'Now you're the enemy.'" I did not hug my brother. What he said pressed deep into my stomach, into the ache there. We said goodnight and parted to our separate bedrooms.

In my own bed, my boyfriend snored lightly, mouth agape in the dark, turned on his side, facing the window that did not have a fire escape. I lied awake for hours, tracing the letters of my name on my enemy's back.

*

I tell too many stories at once. This, too, is a violence. But I want to tell you everything, I want you to love me for it, and I want you to forgive me after I say everything you asked me not to say.

After my mother tried to kill herself in the apartment we shared in Houston, Dustin and I decided on something radical: we asked her to leave, nicely, pained by the conclusion that we all could not live together. We said, take your time, find a place, get on your feet. She said, "I'll be out tomorrow."

My mother left two months later. During that time, she and my father would go out for most of the day and come home with scads of broken-down boxes and salvaged bubble wrap. My father wouldn't talk to Dustin or me, though we kept explaining our stance: how we couldn't keep bounding in through unlocked windows, couldn't keep talking our mother into handing over the gun, couldn't keep holding back her hair as she retches up an overdose. We told him we loved our mother, that we didn't want her to die, but that we couldn't live whole lives around the knives she insisted on wielding.

Boxes lined the kitchen counters. The pressure cooker peeked over the top of one open box, surrounded by guarding soldier-spatulas. My mother entered the kitchen, throwing a plastic utensil into the box, glaring and sniffling in my direction, then retreated to her room. It was impossible to decide which I'd become: guilty ungrateful son or son struggling to be free.

*

A week after I ask my mother to leave she makes me her confidante again. She takes a break from packing the fine unused china stored in the antique wood hutch, which she wraps in a swath of newspaper. We go outside so she can smoke a cigarette. At first our talk is guarded. I stand on the other side of the stairs while my mother sits on a cement step and lights up. Her face is partially concealed by the green-painted steel bars of the railing ascending to the second floor and beyond. The more we talk, the more comfortable we get. She offers me a cigarette out of habit, but I've quit. As she talks, I group her options.

Option 1: She considers leaving my father again for another man. She's thinking of going back to John, but has also met in an online chat room a man named Jesse, a Scorpio who lives in Dallas, works as a computer programmer, and lives in a big pretty house.

Option 2: My parents drive off together. My aunt Karen has promised them the use of her unrented trailer back in Heltonville, Indiana, where they could make a new start.

Option 3: She says she and my father will drive the old rust-stained frozen-odometer Mazda Miata out to the middle of nowhere one night when my brother and me are asleep. She says she'll watch my father shoot himself, then take the gun and commit suicide too. *Won't you be happy as a pig in shit then*, she says.

The sentence starts out as a taunt, but turns serious. She barks out "pig in shit" as our upstairs neighbor, a quiet woman, descends the stairs. The woman's eyes fly open, then back and forth between me and my mother, who turns away with her cigarette. When she's at her car, our petite neighbor yells back at us, "You the pig!" and slams her door. She reverses hard, throws her car into forward and tears off, her wheels leaving tread on the concrete.

Any other time, we'd have burst out laughing, tears rolling down our cheeks as we tried to catch our breath.

*

The first time my mother called to tell me she was going to kill herself, I was nineteen years old. It was March, I was a junior in college. I was on the way to class, anxious about a quiz I hadn't studied for, but answered the phone in a rush. My mother said, "I'm calling to say goodbye."

I didn't know what to do. I thought, *She's got to be kidding*. But then she spilled out the bottle of sleeping pills, her voice unwavering as I could hear them skidding across the bathroom counter. She counted, out loud, by threes. This was happening.

"I just want to go and see my mom," my mother cried. I kept saying, "Take a deep breath." I stalled for time, trying to find the words a boy uses to save his mother. I kept talking until Dustin came home from school to find her with the pills and a loaded revolver on her bed. He called my father, who rushed home early from work.

I failed the quiz.

*

It's impossible to know now, but the one I think of as Attempt # 4 took place in the middle of the night, during another family fight, after one of us kids said

54

The Wrong Thing. Our mother shot up out of her waterbed. She stomped out of her room, matching the volume of her voice to the vehemence of her march. "I'll just go get hit by a car," she yelled back at us. She slammed the front door so hard the windows in her bedroom vibrated.

Yes, way out west in unincorporated Fort Lauderdale, five minutes from the Everglades, at three in the morning, my mother was going to go stand in traffic. I couldn't help picturing her waiting for hours on the dark median on Bonaventure Boulevard. I pictured her, killing time waiting for the Mack truck, drawing and revising her own chalk outline on the asphalt.

My mother wore a powder-blue polyester nightie to go stand in traffic. At 3 a.m. our tiny neighborhood was dark. She was a pearly banshee, hoping for a semi. Our neighbors' sprinklers were timed to go off at this hour, so when my barefoot mother marched out into the night, she got only so far before she slipped. She went down hard, her nightgown flipping up. She remained there sitting, stunned. Then she tried to get up, and fell again, her feet flying out beneath her. Finally, she had to roll on her side over into the grass because she couldn't get a foothold. Dustin trailed after her, but had to turn away so she wouldn't see him laugh.

*

Terror wouldn't exist without comedy in the story of how my mother tries to die.

*

Another attempt—I can't place this in a timeline, only the house in Fort Lauderdale. Am I home on break? Have I graduated? All I know: another fight, this time between my mother and me, and we have gone into our different rooms and then come back together. I find a note she's placed under my father's pillow. I see *pills* and *sorry*, and then I know what I have to do.

I talk her into the bathroom. I don't know how I do it; I am not focusing on what I'm saying, but on the tone. I feel like some professional called in to talk down jumpers. I only know that suddenly I'm holding back her hair in a ponytail while she kneels by the commode, her finger down her throat.

"Oh god, they're white." I don't respond. I've retreated to some place inside of myself, some place where the other versions of Talk-Her-Down-Me congregate and wordlessly implode. "They're *white*," she repeats, hissing out the word. I don't understand the importance until I remember taking one of those blue Tylenol PMs myself. My mother looks up at me, her blue-colored contacts swimming in fear.

I stay with my mother, soothing her, until my father comes home. My father worked at a toxicology laboratory then. He allays any fear that my mother ingested enough of the medicine to really harm her. Still, neither of us lets her fall asleep that night.

*

One failure erases six successes; one bullet, one bottle of pills, one step out into the busy thoroughfare eradicates all those years you loved someone. You don't survive this in one piece. You will never be your mother's savior again. You are descended from a long line of people who do not know that they can live without suffering.

*

My father's voice on the answering machine is slurred, how he talks after his stroke, vowels running into each other like blind ice skaters in warm-up. There's a crispness, too—it takes him so long to say each word, he fights for every syllable. This is what the stroke has done to him, and my mother has wondered, in the emails she sends, if the cyst in his brain isn't pushing on something that slurs his voice.

They live in Heltonville, a tiny rural community in Indiana, a two hours' drive from Indianapolis, in that trailer that Aunt Karen promised them so many years ago. My father's voice on the answering machine is upset. "Can you guys give me a call? It's an emergency." He leaves this kind of message at least once a week. The emergencies have been, over the past few weeks: my uncle refusing to return my father's call, a vandalized car that was probably the handiwork of some teenagers, and, then, this one: my mother took pills as my father watched. Thirty sleeping pills.

Listening to the message again, a voice inside me says, *This will end without you saying goodbye to her.*

But it ends like the rest, only without my being there, enveloped in terror, counting the pills as they slip out of her throat and into the toilet. It ends with the ambulance and the police, with my mother in the back of a squad car, with her on the fifth floor of a hospital, hundreds of miles away.

Or, it doesn't end, not really. It just lives somewhere else, in the place between my heart and stomach, between the ribs. It lives a single life. It never heals. It refuses to die.

Adventures in Old Lady Land

1.

My paternal grandmother lounges comfortably on the orange couch, holding a none-too-pleased, two-year-old version of myself. She's wearing a particularly hideous dress, one that pops up in other photographs of this time. It's a sleeveless, high-neck number, the kind of 1970s garb that forbids cleavage but gives enthusiastic thumbs-up to the hanging gardens of arm flab. Orange, intricate diamonds nearly collide against brown asteroid squares against an eggshell background. I am rebelling against the horror of this fabric,[1] my fist curled up in a ball, near my mouth, my eyes closed. I am red-faced, squirming in a blue baby suit with matching nightcap, which has an attached, fuzzy blue ball that rolls over my forehead. It's that stupid ball which pisses me off as I pose for yet another picture.

---

[1] Years later, I encounter the dress without my grandmother, at a seaside diner in Jensen Beach, Florida. Since then, I cannot look at Grandma's clothes without thinking "tablecloth."

Other interpretations exist. My mother swears I was teething. My father testifies that he waited in the wings with a bottle to feed me, and that I could become unruly when hungry. I prefer my own versions. There are four.

A).   They are interrupting *The Sonny & Cher Comedy Hour* and I am missing the debut of Bob Mackey's newest creation. If only I could write and describe my newborn fashion plight to Bob and Cher—I just know they'd rescue me.

B).   Besides being circulated from adult to adult while people eat *my cake*, I am upset about the conundrum that has thrown the drag queens at the Vatican into an uproar. Pope Paul VI, who kind of resembles Cher's mother, has been dead for just a little over two months, at the ripe old-lady age of eighty. The new pope, John Paul I, retired by way of coffin after just thirty-four days in office at the age sixty-five, much to everyone's surprise. John I was succeeded by Cardinal Karol Wojtyla, who morphed into the healthy-as-a-horse John Paul II. On what was only my second birthday. You'd cry too.

C).   I am doing my best to "make a scene." I have found that I am unusually proficient at this. My resume already includes the ability to holler at the top of my lungs for ten hours, a feat achieved when my family moved from Brownstown, Indiana, to our now-home of DeLand, Florida, just a little over a year ago. It wasn't that I was unhappy to leave Indiana. Please. At one year old, I'd seen the Barnett Bank, inhaled the dust from America's finest dirt roads, visited the movie theater, participated in Sunday morning sessions of kitchen gossip. I had done all there was to do. With such raw ability on my side, I figured I'd be a shoe-in for 1978's Best Actress Award. Screw ugly Diane Keaton and her owl glasses.

D). Grandma smells. It is said of her, in hushed tones and behind her back, mainly by my mother, that she "can knock a buzzard off a shitwagon."

I cannot show this picture to Grandma. On the stage that is the photograph, her scene-making is far more studied. Her performance is subtle, yet shocking. While what the audience first sees is me in a heartbreaking adaptation of *Tantrum*, what arrests attention is the fact that my grandmother doesn't wear any underwear.

2.

My love of old lady regalia started young, as documented by an early photograph of me in grandma garb. If I had written the caption, it'd read, "Our model sports a sassy, dark blue sweater, pulled tight over this fall's hottest huntress green negligee, with matching gossamer scarf and slip." The negligee, six-year-old me decides, is less bedwear than ball gown. I have on all manner of primary-colored plastic necklaces and false-gold clip-on earrings. My cheeks shine with rouge. My eyelids wink in an angelic pink hue, and my lips say *emergency!* with color. No one has helped me.[2] It is a wonder I can hold up my head, which is adorned with the most fabulous item my grandmother ever owned: a faux-fur leopard-print pillbox hat, which is too big for me, so it nearly swallows my head. Pillbox hats and leopard print are both institutions

---

[2] I embody an argument for the genetic origins of drag.

I am desperate to understand. On the back of the photograph, Grandma has scrawled: "Our little Zsa Zsa, 1984."

3.

I am disallowed from telling Grandma about my homosexuality. Even if I wanted to share its toys, I can't. My father absolutely forbids it. In the colossal argument we had in 1998 when I said I wanted to tell Grandma, he screamed at me, "Why would you want to do that to an old lady?" I didn't miss a beat when I yelled back, "For kicks!"

4.

Grandma lives in Homestead, Florida. She rents out the empty bedrooms in her home, and one of these renters becomes what she calls her fourth grandson. "He's so much like you and Dustin," she says to me. We notice that Grandson #4 is never like CJ, our older brother whose girlfriends Grandma always dislikes. Number 4 is "handsome" and "so sensitive!" Ray Gonzales works construction and treats my grandmother like his own. He even calls her "Grandma Hall." She gives examples: "'Now Grandma Hall,' he'll say, 'don't you lift that box. You let me do it.'"[3]

---

[3] Grandma's voice sounds a lot like Edith Bunker has taken a bong hit of helium.

She always laughs an exuberant old-lady-doted-upon-by-a-cute-hardbodied-young'n laugh and nudges my arm while extolling his virtues. I have the distinct feeling she's setting me up.

She continues her surreptitious matchmaking for about a year. Once, when she drove from Homestead to Daytona Beach (a good day's drive), she called and asked me to let Ray know that she was okay.[4] I deepened my voice for the occasion. He sounded sufficiently impressed. And very, very gay. Another time, she invited me to a basketball game: "Ray will drive, and afterwards we'll get ice cream." I declined. I'd had few dates, and they went wrong enough without my grandmother orchestrating the adventure.[5]

A few months after that, my mother stopped by Grandma's house on her way back up from the Keys. Ray was shirtless in the backyard with an equally shirtless friend, working on his truck. My mother stood a safe distance away from Grandma and as they spoke the conversation turned to Grandson #4. "You know Marsha," Grandma said, not lowering her voice, "I think Ray's gay." She said it flatly, without any hint of epiphany. "Before you leave I want to show you my new gladiolas."

I know a few things from this incident. I know my grandmother uses without shame the term *gay*. And, what's more, I know Grandma thinks she

---

[4] My parents owned a courier service with a nationwide 800 number, and Grandma is "frugal." So her maneuver here is less matchmaker and more Pennysaver.

[5] Now that I think of it, maybe if Grandma had escorted my date with E.T., he probably wouldn't have felt so free to say, "I want to put it in your bellybutton," when I asked him what he wanted to do after dinner.

knows what kind of guys I'm into. Apparently, I like slightly older, fey-mannered, Latino construction workers who shave their legs and chests.[6]

I also know that my love life has effectively flatlined.

5.

Old ladies outnumber old gentlemen by about five and a half million in America.[7] That leaves about one and one-half grandmas for every grandpa in the United States. So it's strange when I see a picture of Grandma surrounded by five old guys, each holding an outstretched bowling ball as if in offering, each wearing an electric blue jacket with the name *Betty's Guys* in gold thread over the chest. Grandma's full name is Ruth-Betty and suffice it to say, either Grandma is the most popular woman at the Homestead Bowling Lanes, or she's the only woman who'll bowl two times every week, year-round. Old ladies outnumber their male counterparts because men over the age of sixty-five make up 85 percent of elderly suicides,[8] a fact I corroborate with a cutout from the *Miami Herald* that Grandma sent me. It's a picture of an event held at Homestead's senior center,

---

[6] Pretty accurate so far.

[7] According to the 2010 U.S. Census (in which Grandma forgot to participate), women comprise 22,905,024 of the total 40,267,984 Americans over the age of sixty-five (http://factfinder.census.gov).

[8] Rates are highest in Montana (http://suicidology.org).

a picture consisting of only women. There's not a representative of Betty's Guys to be seen. This is the senior center's annual picnic, and no one seems to have an opposite-gendered date. Grandma stands in the foreground and has marked herself by putting XXX on the hem of her shorts, uncomfortably near her crotch, so that we, her grandsons, might find her.

6.

In 1999, my grandmother becomes embroiled in some considerable lesbian intrigue. It starts because of her friendship with Esther2. Esther2 is a loud-mouthed, big-nosed broad, whom Grandma befriends in the Senior Center Bridge Clan.[9] She lives in a retirement community, where she makes lots of friends because, she says, "I'll talk to anyone, I don't care."

Our first introduction to Esther2 comes Christmas Day, 1999. Throughout the day, Esther evinces an absentmindedness that compares only to my dead grandfather's. She leaves her glasses on tables, on seats, and behind the Listerine underneath the bathroom sink. In the space of that first day, she tells the same story of driving to Vermont three times. Each time her voice tinges with excitement; the memory is new, even if the language isn't. I adore Esther, her translucent white beehive, and especially her spectacular outbursts

---

[9] Esther1 died of lung cancer the year before Grandma met Esther2. Esther1 possessed a foul mouth and a quick wit. If there's an old lady besides Grandma I'd like to be, it's Esther1.

of incredible volume. When Grandma guesses that Esther doesn't like stuffing (because she passed that dish without even looking at it), she yells out, "I! Didn't! Say! That! I like mashed potatoes. Just! Fine!"

But I really fall for Esther during her story of the woman who has keyed Grandma's car: "She lives in the next building over; we have a parking lot in common. Well, we made chitchat one day out there near our cars. I was coming home from bridge, and she was just back from the market. She seemed nice. We got to talking about how lonely this place can get. She wished she could find someone to go to church with. But she was too shy. I said, 'I'll go with you, I don't mind.' I'll talk to anyone, I don't care. Don't interrupt."

"Sunday, we go to church. Lovely service, lots of hymns. Afterwards I start talking to some of these people and introduce her. I'll talk to anyone. But she didn't want to talk. She just stood there in the corner. Don't interrupt! Afterwards, we go to Denny's for brunch. I always have the American Slam. And she breaks down crying. 'I wish I could be like you, Esther,' she says, 'I'll never make friends.' I felt so bad for her, we became friends. But she's ... needy. That's it, that's the story."

I've been trying to ascertain what kind of church they went to. And Esther has been stalling. Now that she's finished, I ask outright. Esther's face flushes. She begins twirling her long necklace around one finger. "Well, it was a ... *gay* church. I'll talk to anyone, I don't care, I was just trying to help her find *friends*." Esther2's face turns solid-as-stone. She stutters up the cathedral-sized steps of "gay," but ultimately triumphs. She has spunk. After all, she's attended a queer church.

Esther's friendship with Grandma sparks the neighbor's jealousy. At first, the neighbor puts notes that read "You leave her alone" under the wiper on Grandma's car. Now, she has etched "bitch" onto the hood with a key. "My grandmother, the Other Woman," I say out loud. Grandma smirks back and says, "Who knew?"

7.

Grandma sits on my bed, looking out two large windows that face west and crowd the small room with heat. Sweat makes its way down my back, making me even more uncomfortable to be standing next to Grandma as she sobs into my mom's shoulder.

When I was a kid, I used to stand on the chairs at Grandma's table and yell, "Dee Dee died!" I don't know why I found it worth announcing that my grandmother's mother was dead, except that it made Grandma run from the room in tears. Power leaked from her as she left the room.

Now, however, I don't want anything to do with this brittle ascension of pain. My mother sits with her arm around my grandma. I stand behind them, in what feels like an annex. I am just a visitor to Old Lady Land, mere witness to actual grief, and the carpet I stand on feels detached before the matriarch. It's 1993 and my grandfather has been dead for six hours. My brother and I were in school when my mother pulled us out. We drove down to Homestead to collect her. There, beside the house they lived in, a white sheet billowed over Grandpa's body. I could see the hammer that died in his hands the instant before he fell to the ground.[10]

My grandmother says she heard him say "shit" really loudly, "Like he was about to complain something was left out, and then he just fell." Grandma tucks a used Kleenex into the wristband of her watch, and uses a clean one to blow her nose. I have a deep anxiety about her sitting on my bed, because, and I don't mean to be indelicate, she *smells*. She substitutes a dip in the neighbor's overchlorinated pool for showers. Her teeth are different colors. We have to wipe down the phone with antiseptic to remove the odor she leaves there with her breath. I have just seen *Aliens* with Sigourney Weaver and imagine Grandma's stench eats through my comforter much like the aliens' blood corrodes human skin. My mother looks hard at me, and I put an arm around my crying grandma. I feel the heat in her bare arms. I see the moist handkerchief in her hand. I see my grandmother's mouth open, wordless. She raises her head, takes a big breath, and shouts: "We hadn't had sex in eight years!"

8.

Grandma makes people take lots of photographs of her and sometimes she'll send me some, now that we don't see each other very often. The unfortunate

---

[10] In 1993, I was the only junior in Mrs. Adas's freshman health class. I completed CPR certification a week before Grandpa died of a heart attack. For months, I felt guilty, convinced I could have saved his life.

part of this arrangement is that they are given in lieu of cash or t-shirts from her travels or even that grandma standby, the ten-pack of tube socks. For Yule 2001, several five-by-seven reproductions of the same image arrive: Grandma on a 4x4 off-road vehicle. Behind her, a man that looks stunningly like, but is not, my grandfather winks into the camera.[11] Grandma accompanied a friend to New Jersey just before September 11th, and when all air travel was frozen, they stayed at the friend's relative's house. Grandpa Lookalike is about to give my smiling grandmother a tour of the acreage. Grandma has made sure that the event is memorialized, because she takes great pleasure in the fact that she remains active at eighty-four. I do too. Her "schedule" pinned up on my refrigerator details two bowling teams (despite arthritis), three days of volunteering at the senior center, and a bridge clan she won't miss for the world.

In another photograph, she wears fading blue shorts, a blue-and-white sleeveless shirt, and a beaded necklace that descends to her waistline. Her pocketbook seems fashioned out of wicker and rests delicately in the cranny made by her elbow, bent just shy of a right angle. Her left hand rests on a trash can. There is no indication about what exactly is thrilling about garbage. Grandma *is* a recycling fanatic, but she neither gestures at the receptacle nor seems to notice that it is a trash can she has her hand upon.

She is art-for-art's-sake.

For my birthday last year, my grandmother gave me pictures of

---

[11] When Dustin sees the picture, he mocks indignation: "Hey! Who's that guy giving Grandma some backdoor action?"

herself dressed as a cavewoman; she wears a pleated brown skirt and a chee-tah-print blouse. A headband cut from the same cheetah cloth and knotted above her right ear guarantees the outfit's spotlit place in the Grandma Getups Hall of Fame. She is less a geriatric prostitute than an eighties aerobic instruc-tor, and there's something about the pleats that *really* work for her. Bitch.

9.

One summer, when I am ten, my parents send my brothers and me to my grandparents in Homestead. We are there to pick lychees. Grandma's backyard is an orchard of these exotic trees, which bear a reddish purple fruit. Mostly, lychees are used in Asian cuisine, sometimes in fried rice dishes or served in heavy syrup as dessert. My brothers and I spend days on rickety ladders secured to the tops of rusty vans, reaching into hornet-ridden branches, picking bucket-fuls of dull red fruit. We refer to this period as Our Summer of Hell. Each day, Grandma marches us into the orchard.

At dinnertime, my older brother hides deep inside that thicket; it protects him from what awaits at the supper table. Most nights we dine on limpid spaghetti, baked in a watery Ragu sauce and served alongside some-thing Grandpa calls monkey burgers, which are lumps of baked meat that I eat with lots of ketchup. There's always plenty of stale white bread and a tub of margarine. One night, instead of the bitter fruit for dessert, Grandma makes pudding. A look of dread passes between Dustin and me. Grandpa is diabetic.

The pudding is sugarless.

Luckily, Grandma has to go to the store. She doles out the sugarless chocolate punishment into wooden bowls, one for each of us. She eats hers standing, then says, "Hurry, Dustin, so we can get to Publix." She scrapes the spoon against the bottom of the bowl, puts her dish down, and walks away. It's then, even before she has left the dining room, that she takes off her shorts.

Grandpa calls after her, "Are you in a hurry?" Grandma does not get the joke. What's worse: she turns around.

"What?"

Grandpa says, more urgently, "Is it too hot in here?" He stares at her naked crotch, then at us, then back at her.

"Johnny, you're so *crazy*. Take your medicine! Come on, Dusty, eat your pudding!"

Dustin devours his pudding, washing it down with the generic-label strawberry soda she only lets us drink with dinner.

When the door shuts, I grab the bowl and shovel the brown, lumpy paste back into its source. I am so grateful for this reprieve that I don't remember that Grandpa is at the table too. I feel his heavy glare. I turn to him, and his head is cocked to one side, his mouth slightly open. His eyes sparkle blue judgment. He hands me his untouched bowl and gestures for me to empty his too.

"Tastes like shit, doesn't it?" He winks.[12]

----

[12] We never speak of this again. Evil Naked Grandma has been thwarted.

10.

"Grandma, Jamie wants to know what *douche* means," Dustin says over a game of rummy one of those summer nights. We are eight and nine years old. My face takes on the icy quality of sherbet. Suddenly the word I've been repeating in my head for days has been tossed into my face, along with Grandma's suspicious look.

Dustin is telling the truth. I would very much like to know what *douche* means, ever since we saw a late-night commercial for something called O.B. in Disguise. I've been walking around Grandma's house singing the O.B. jingle.

Grandma almost spills her coffee and locks eyes with me.

She clears her throat. She finishes her coffee, sets the cup on the saucer. She acts as if no one has said anything even remotely related to vaginas or the fact that they might require the use of specialized tools.

Then she says, "It's a soap women use *down there* so it doesn't burn." She looks at me. Then, suddenly, she smiles, as if she can see—sensitive fashion savant who steals her pillbox hats, devoted diarist of her every photographed public appearance, man who will never need this information in his natural-born gay life—what the future will make of me.

11.

Bereft of the metaphoric powers granted the young and smooth, old lady flesh points at futurity and the atrophy inherent in transformation. Old ladies do not signal lust except in comic situations. They are not allowed to board the rides in the Land of Desire.[13]

During what is now a famous speech, the late French feminist Monique Wittig was asked by an audience member if she had a vagina. She emphatically responded, "No." Sex organs—dubbed "reproductive organs" in my college biology textbook—have been constituted not as mediums of women's pleasure, but as centers for oppression. Because the vagina does not exist outside of procreation, old ladies are vagina-free.[14] Their sexual identity lasts until the onset of menopause, a phenomenon which seems, if Grandpa is any indication of the elderly heterosexual male population, aptly named.

I remember Grandma once answering her door while still buttoning her shirt. As someone who has been shocked awake by my grandmother's naked torso, I empathized with the person who was about to be confronted by old lady

---

[13] Young old coupling is always laughable in our culture. Besides the slew of films like *Harold and Maude*, consider one Snickers commercial, in which a college-aged man helps an old woman cross a street then asks if she's free Saturday night. The announcer states the moral: "Impaired judgment: another unfortunate side effect of hunger." Old Ladies only exist on the sexual menu to incite laughter.

[14] There is no such thing as "vagina envy" in Freud or Lacan, both of whom argue that the lack of penis shapes female subjectivity. Males are not determined by their lack of vagina. Not until high school, at least.

bosom. Grandma is not a mentally slow woman. She may not have the best of hearing these days, but she's not absent-minded. I can only reckon that Grandma has internalized the fact that her body no longer functions in terms that anyone cares to notice, and so her body overthrows shame. She opened the door, and the Jehovah's Witness on her stoop coughed twice before he found the breath to offer her the latest issue of *The Watchtower*.

I understand why the realization that she hadn't had sex in eight years came the day that Grandpa died. The exile Grandma had feared for so long was happening: she'd never make love with her husband again; perhaps she'd never be intimate with anyone ever again. Perhaps now no one would want her. My grandma, maybe, was no longer a woman at all.

12.

Grandma is a hunky football player whose eye black grease shines in wide swaths beneath her laughing eyes. She wears someone's frayed Dolphins jersey and her shoulder pads rise to earlobes she's adorned with clip-ons. She tucks the football between breast and armpit. Grandma is what I could never be: an All-American transvestite jock.

This is Grandma's 2003 Yuletide photograph, and she sends three of them, along with gifts, to me, Dustin, and Brandon.[15] Brandon has never

---

[15] Grandma met Brandon the previous summer, when my father fell into a coma. After spending the day at the hospital, Grandma and Brandon watched the Little League World Series at

received a Grandma gift and does not understand why we are giddy. I unwrap a weather-beaten cardboard box so threadbare it reveals its contents. I pull out a dirty plastic manger complete with dirty plastic Baby Jesus and a Virgin Mary whose wires show underneath her faded blue plastic dress. These light-up lawn arrangements, Grandma has written on a note inside, once belonged to her neighbor, now deceased. She also notes that Mary's wiring may need reworking before I am able to "turn her on."

Dustin opens his package and starts laughing so quickly that Brandon and I wonder what pilfered remnant of a dead lady's estate he's received. He turns it around to show an enlarged magazine cover, laminated and cheaply framed. Nineteen-year-old Dustin smiles at us in a tuxedo jacket, his red silk bowtie almost sparkling. Embracing him from behind is an equally tuxedoed man. The man's blonde coiffure is as impeccably groomed as Dustin's jet-black hair. He rests his head on Dustin's shoulder, his cheek grazing Dustin's. And if one had any doubts as to these two hunky models' sexuality, the cover states that this particular publication is "South Florida's Gay Community Newspaper."[16] This was a publicity photo for the first

night. Their friendly banter restored us to the life where people still played games and no one's father was going to die. Brandon called Grandma "my favorite Hall." When I said, "Besides me," he repeated: "My favorite Hall."

[16] *The Weekly News* was founded in August of 1977 by volunteers working against the campaign former beauty queen Anita Bryant was waging to repeal the first pro-gay human rights ordinance passed in Dade County (she won that fight). This is Dustin's second cover. His first was for *TWN*'s Mother's Day issue; on that cover, my mother and he compose an epitome of the gay-friendly American family. *TWN* ceased publication in 2006.

annual Gay Youth Prom, an event Dustin and his photogenic companion, Dale Ayres, engineered for Dade and Broward Counties' queer eighteen-to-twenty-five-year-olds. Grandma has rummaged through our storage unit in Florida for her upcoming garage sale to benefit Betty's Guys. Clearly, this photograph documents a valuable event in Dustin's emotional life, and her gift is recognition made without judgment.

A week later, when I call to thank her for the presents, Grandma answers out of breath. She explains that she's been in her greenhouse "playing in the dirt."[17] I can see her arthritic hands wrist-deep in a mound of mulch, weeding out unwanted debris. After thanking her for her thoughtful gifts, I tell my eighty-six-year-old grandmother that Grandsons #2 and #3 are gay.

Grandma says, "Uh-huh" and pauses. Her silence stretches longer than I'd hoped, and I can hear her switch the phone to the other ear. I'm not even sure she has heard me until she finally sighs and says, "Well, so what?"

I always thought I'd have to dispel for Grandma the negative but enduring notions of "the gay lifestyle"—exotic drugs made from animal tranquilizers, weeknight orgies with leathermen, the requisite drag queen career. But it's me who is guilty of stereotyping. The "damage control" I've had to do with other relatives and friends is unnecessary. There is no ruin between us.

Still, I am amazed by her cavalier attitude. She says into my silence,

---

[17] Runner-up for eyebrow-lifting grandma entendre. The reigning champion comes from the conversation in which Grandma says that after waking up she spends an hour or so "fooling around with myself in the bed."

"I had a long inkling." We both chuckle at this, relieved. Then Grandma says, "When I was a girl, there were no Black people in my neighborhood." I'm not sure how to respond, so I don't. Grandma continues. "That was my generation's trouble. I think being gay is your generation's." She bridges us by making the same racial-model argument common to LGBT activists working to gain protected status for American sexual minorities. We are queer heroes of social justice, she implies, knowing that I remember her volunteer work at the DeLand welfare office when I was a child. She concludes, "I don't see anything wrong with being gay."

We reach the end of our talk. Grandma never says "I love you" on the phone, and the times I've said it to her, she responded with a politely grunted "Uh huh" as the phone fell on its hook. I decide to risk the sentimentality. Grandma does not let me down. She grunts her vague acknowledgment as the phone begins its descent. But then the phone rises back up. Without asking if I'm still there, she says, "I love you too, Jamie." Then she hangs up.

She returns to planting flowers in green pots, covering them with handfuls of dirt. In a month or two, her impatiens will blossom, and she'll hand them out as Easter gifts to her friends at the senior center. I wonder how they'll feel, receiving my grandmother's annuals on a holiday that is ubiquitously celebrated by chocolate confections. I wonder if they understand Grandma as more than their bowling or bridge partner, more than the president of the Florida Lychee Grower's Association, more than a widow whose free time is spent playing in the dirt. I wonder if they see her as I do: a landscape alive with color, resisting a cartographer's quick sketches.

My AIDS

One of the things that separate us from our ancestors and make contemporary experience profoundly different from that of other ages is the disappearance of epidemic disease as a serious factor in human life.

—William H. McNeill, author of *Plagues and Peoples*, in *The New York Review of Books*, (July 21, 1983).[1]

The first major illness known by an acronym, the condition called AIDS does not have, as it were, natural borders. It is an illness whose identity is designed for purposes of investigation, tabulation, and surveillance. . . .

—Susan Sontag, *AIDS and Its Metaphors*

1.

Outside the tent, on stage, all three hundred pounds of operatic Martha Wash

conspire with prerecorded bass and electronica to begin Gay Pride 1998. Drag

---

[1] Quoted by Sontag in *AIDS and Its Metaphors*.

queens in white tutus provide the organized impossibility of cancan. Behind them, Latino men in pink g-strings and angel wings pose and throw glitter into softly whirring fans. I dodge the blue flash of fairy dust. I avoid the urinals lining the edges of the park. I avoid brushing up against men without shirts or jeans; avert my gaze from bare, hairy chests and jockstrapped butts. Until one man, who appears in glossy ads for a bar called The Ramrod in the gay weeklies I've recently begun reading, walks by in nothing but blue onionskin shorts. With every step, his penis bobs left then right, tenting the cloth in front a good three inches. I am an uneasy solution of salty disgust and piercing attraction.

Inside, the tent muffles the music. Men remove their shirts from belt loops and put them on again. Men and women, some together, others alone, move along various rows. I do not look at them. I am nineteen, discovering AIDS.

The panels are each three feet by six feet, hand-stitched, some comprising just names and dates. More elaborate ones include poems, obits, photographs. One specific cluster of names draws my attention. These men are on first-name basis, laid out so that each touches a center panel. *COURAGE* radiates in yellow against a regal blue background.

AIDS unthreads its victims, but here they are sewn back together. Looking at these tapestries forced to testify, I'm not sure which face represents Courage. Is he the bearded wannabe-biker still straddling his Harley, so full-bodied that his chaps cannot contain him? Or is he the book-thin, nerdy, button-down Eddie Bauer model, surprised by the flash at his desk? Haphazard photographers have stitched film into fabric. No dates frame these bodies. Sometimes, hair tells time: this one's leonine mullet acid-rocks its way through the seventies, this one's hairsprayed helmet promotes big-business eighties. But, mostly, they died at every moment.

When I exit the tent, the music mixes with light. I am monochrome under an impressive clear sky. The parade of men keeps marching. I am afraid to look at its body parts.

2.

My brother revealed he was gay at home over Taco Bell. My mother couldn't finish eating her Burrito Supreme and started crying. Later that night, she told my father, and he cried too. They believed, at first, that Dustin wasn't gay—he was under the influence of some faggot mafia. I remember my father's attitude during the first days. From the basement phone in Flagler Hall, near the computer lab where I spent most of my freshman year, I called my parents to tell them I had gotten an A on a religion test and my dad said, *Your brother isn't gay. It's those faggots turning him.* My mother believed it too. They taped his conversations and refused to let him out of the house. He was Misfit-Mafioso-Dustin, and they were on to him.[2]

---

[2] Today, searching for music to listen to while writing this, I uncover one of the tapes that holds Dustin's voice from back then. But he is chipmunked, chirping too fast. The past moves at such pace; I have to slow it down.

It was 1994. AIDS had been news for fourteen years; the Quilt had been nominated for the Nobel Peace Prize five years earlier, the once-ubiquitous t-shirt "Silence = Death" had faded. But my mother, who will admit to perfect strangers that she can't do fractions, worked out some infallible formula where GAY = AIDS. A week before Dustin's birthday, she loaded the .22 pistol. She wrote notes. She wouldn't let Dustin suffer.

I called that afternoon. We toured again the already well-worn paths owned by New Dustin. We reached the cliff overlooking the war-torn geography of Old Dustin. I kept telling her that he wasn't irreconcilably ceded from the union. I said, in a gently exasperated voice, "Mom, you don't get AIDS just by coming out of the closet."

I didn't know: she was sitting on the edge of her bed, working up the courage to kill my brother.

3.

I learned the erotics of fear from Jeremy and Danny, in speech class, tenth grade. They both played football. Jeremy's broad shoulders, brown eyes and deep voice mesmerized me. I had two classes with him that year. He slept through history. But in speech, his tongue activated, licked its lips at me, knowing somehow I was watching. I wasn't the only one always looking at him: the girls in the class fawned over him. Allison crossed the room to bring him paper; Heather carried an array of extra pens just for him; Aimee lugged his book in her backpack. Free from all burdens, Jeremy existed carefree under desire's stare.

Danny was John Stamos's better-looking, rounder-assed clone. His dimples wanted to be nice to me. But two cruel lines formed his mouth. Danny's last name was Comer, which is Spanish for "to eat," which is exactly what I wanted to do to him.

Jeremy and Danny would sit as close as possible to me. They'd nudge me. They'd whisper to each other while looking at me then say: *We've decided to let you come watch us fuck after school.* They'd smack each other lightly on the upper arm with the back of limp wrists. I listened to the smack, its double prophecy. First, skin on skin, desire rappelling down the chiseled mountain of flesh. Then the darker, louder vision of lesion-purple eyes, bloodied mouth. They'd lisp through sentences like, *It'th your turn to make me your bit-th. I fucked you latht night.* I tried making my face into stone. The effort showed. Jeremy took to calling me "AIDS boy."

I wanted to say: *YES. I'm gay. I'll meet you at your house. Make sure you're all lubed up.* But I feared what monster would replace the one I only had to endure for an hour.

After speech class, I went to the bathroom and masturbated furiously.[3]

---

[3] Jeremy died in a car crash that year. In both classes, girls wept all hour long. Teachers gave us the entire period off, "to reflect." In speech, Allison, Heather, and Aimee's eyes appeared puffy, their faces choked with emotion. I don't remember Danny being there that day; his sister Rachel had been in the same car as Jeremy but had survived. A banner hung in the halls reading, *We will remember you, Jeremy Fradin.* The yearbook staff planned a memorial page. The football coach read an elegy over the P.A. But me: I was glad.

4.

The first time Dustin was tested for HIV, he did it because his friends were nervous about going to the clinic. So, a blood-sister pact of a new kind was made. They did their hair and wore Lycra shirts to the clinic. When Dustin told the woman administering a battery of very personal questions that he was a virgin, she said, "Sugar, why are you here?"

I helped calm his nerves by telling him a smattering of narratives that Dustin took to calling *The Ben And Michelle Saga*. These emails told the tale of Ben, my roommate, and his girlfriend, Michelle, an overweight, ex-anorexic drama queen who turned down, she said, a full scholarship to Duke to follow a guy to Orlando where he dumped her when she became "preg-a-nant." Michelle had recently focused her obsessive stare on me. She lurked outside my classes. She mysteriously materialized at restaurants. She suggested I join her and Ben for threeways.

She once solicited advice from me and my best friend, Chi, at an IHOP, only to interrupt our conversation to let us know, "There's a *black* family sitting behind you now." She said the word "black" smaller and with her hand half-covering her mouth. She said "black" to the "gay" and the "Asian," neither of whom were "amused." Michelle had just found out that her father, who died when she was young, was HIV positive and gay. She took care to mention my likeness to him whenever she ambushed me. *You're just like my dad*, she'd say, slipping into the seat across from me at Denny's, as I lifted a forkful of eggs to my mouth and wondered how the hell she'd found me this time. *He ate just like that too.* Besides his eccentric habit of using silverware, apparently I also shared the man's jawline and bottom teeth, as well as an erotic attraction for people of the same gender. I even danced like him, as Michelle noted the only time I ever took her and Ben to The Barracks, a military-themed gay bar whose only real parallel with the paradigmatic paratrooper was a challenged sense of bathroom cleanliness.

I am pretty sure Michelle made most of this up. But that didn't stop her from believing herself. When I told Michelle about Johnny,[4] she looked me up and down, sadly, as if she wanted to remember me this way instead of how I'd look in the future, staring back from a hospital bed …. "I don't want you to end up like my dad," she said. "He isn't 'black' is he?"

My apparent resemblance of a man whose death was HIV linked, and other of Michelle's racist delusions, took Dustin's mind off his own agonizing, two-week wait. His favorite episode was the one where Michelle confronted me about my plan to move out. A week before, incensed by my re-fusal to come home one night, she had written *AIDS faggot!* across poems and photographs; had torn up reams of research for a paper on Tennyson; had cut (eaten?) some of my clothes right from my closet. I was moving out so this JC-Penny's-feasting wildebeest would never again be tempted by my sweet-smell-ing wardrobe. Michelle wanted to cure the rift and was in the process of convincing me when Chi appeared outside the window behind her.

_____

[4] Hairy back, three dates, HIV-negative. The most he ever did was kiss me awkwardly on the neck.

Chi began mocking Michelle, her face morphing from half-French, half-Chinese to South Carolina psycho in seconds. Her eyes crossed, her mouth slightly slack, her stance just a bit too stolid, Chi looked like Michelle's thinner, long-lost Asian twin. Every time Michelle used the back of her hand to wipe her nose, Chi imitated the motion, then licked her hand. Her eyes rolled up into her head as she imagined the sweet ecstasy of Michelle snot. It was during one of these ecstatic tastings that Michelle turned around and saw Chi performing her. They stared at each other for a minute, then Chi stuck out her tongue and I ran for the door.

Dustin loved this particular story. He emailed me back from the University of Miami computer labs: "The girl next to me thinks I'm a freak, I'm laughing so hard."

The results came back negative. When his overjoyed email reached me, I wrote back, "Of *course* it's negative, dumbass!" I was exasperated at my brother's anxiety; there were real people at real risk, and he, who had just turned eighteen and had barely held a man's hand, had the audacity to appropriate this disease for himself?

But the person I wanted to admonish was me. At night, my brother's face, en media plague, floated expressionless, eyes closed, in front of me, inside a coffin. Until my roommate's face replaced my brother's, and I could hear Ben telling me to wake up, it was a dream.

AIDS saturated the fear in my body, which, evidently, had already succumbed to the disease in a parallel life. How much of Michelle's psychosis was Cassandra at the walls, prophesying demise?

5.

Jake was the first Virgo man I loved. We don't speak now. I've relegated him to memory: the photograph he faxed has curled and yellowed. I tell people it didn't work because he said that *Boys Don't Cry* was "so Hollywood" in the same breath he quoted from *Gladiator*. I tell people it's because he called the transgender body one of "choice" and thus leagues away from that of the homosexual. But the truth contains the following facts:

- He lived in a ranch-style house in Lathrup Village, Michigan. *You live in a place called Throwup Village?* I teased. I lived in South Florida, and though he offered to fly down every weekend, somehow the prospect of a Saturday/Sunday boyfriend didn't thrill. Especially one that wanted to take me to Mass, pray for our sins, then back to the Hotel Six for a little game of "swallow the wafer." No thanks.

- I was already in love with Pete, the fourth June Gemini I'd fallen for. We may have been *just friends*, but I harbored hopes.

- I was twenty-three. Jake was thirty-two … for about 3 weeks. Then he was thirty-four. For another week. We finally settled on thirty-five, although I have no clue if that was his actual age.

One night, Jake tells me a story about the last time he saw his ex, Charles.

While they were both in Paris for work, Charles called and asked him to meet him on a certain bridge at a certain time. It was 1983: *The bridge had a breathtaking view of Notre Dame, which Charles knew I loved. He held out a gold necklace, a cross; he turned me around and put it on my neck. He kissed my neck and said I restored his faith.* Jake's voice goes far away when he tells the story. The travel costs him something in terms of coherence. His voice breaks; suddenly Charles is hospitalized, dying. Jake is on the phone with Charles's father, who says, *I don't have a son; he died a long time ago.* Jake lies to Charles: *Your father is coming, just hold on.* Charles's father does arrive, but too late.

A few days later, I am driving home, my window down, cigarette smoke spilling out of my mouth, diffusing into dusk. Maybe it is the wind that knows, that tells me. Maybe a particle of light has traveled from Throwup Village to Florida in order to relay the news. I don't know how, but I know beyond shadow: the man I am falling in love with over the telephone is positive.

I ask him that night on the phone. He emits a little laugh: *Of course not.* My brow furrows as I retrace my steps. Then, into my silence, he says, "Wait. Yes. I'm sorry."

Friends have told me what to do in this situation.[5] John, brave enough to shave his own asshole, tells me, "I can't deal with poz guys. It grosses me out. I even told that guy Daniel I didn't think we should see each other any more when he told me he was HIV." I just thought Daniel wasn't around anymore because he'd come to his senses about John; I didn't know he was positive.

---

[5] They say, "In This Situation," like it refers to nuclear war. Always in fear of the radioactive.

Steve, who is almost twenty-seven, helped his lover die: "Don't go through it if you don't have to," he says, running his hand through hair that has been gray for years. *In this situation: run.*

I told Jake I didn't care.

Jake's first name is actually Gary, a name he associates with an overweight, bespectacled boy whose high school classmates despised him. I have sympathy for Gary, especially when Jake growls at me, "I won't ever be that boy for anyone again." I am humbled, confused: it's the potato-bodied unpopular boy in high school and not the man whose lover gives him HIV on a bridge that Jake regrets being.

6a.

I read names on a site called *My Dead Friends Page*. At least seventy names in white letters loom against the black screen. All men, sentenced by past tense: *Daniel was a .... Oscar died in ....* Then: *Steven typed in all CAPS in the AIDS echo on Fidonet because his eyes were failing ....* Somehow, Steven is kept alive by *failing*, even though *typed* tells me his voice has long since ceased its trembling echo. Some names take me to other sites where they blossom into photographs. I have spent hours reading elegies for friends and lovers, angers at pharmaceutical companies. Sometimes I look for Jake's name. Last year, his website stopped loading. I am entering into a relationship with the dead.[6]

---

[6] "Reading can, and should, be understood as a practice of mourning." Ross Chambers, *Facing It: AIDS Diaries and the Death of the Author.* (Ann Arbor: University of Michigan, 2001), ix.

These names call for reinscription. I wonder who has said each name, with passion and conviction, pleadingly, angrily… Names curling under in the dirt, turning to dust. I say them aloud to uncaring air until the emptiness is filled. *Tom. Sergei. Jesus.* I don't pause, barely take the breath required. I keep them alive. But, every time my lips finish, they die again. I cannot say them enough.

6b.

I ache for transformation, for the dead to visit. By coming out, I admit to decay. I am admitted into the time-honored tradition of "risk-group—that neutral-sounding, bureaucratic category which also revives the archaic idea of a tainted community that illness has judged."[7] My blood is *sangra non grata* with the Red Cross in 1997, the year I come out. No tests needed; I am a "male who has had sex with another male since 1977," am thus equivalent to someone who has:

- used a needle, even once, to take drugs or steroids not prescribed by a physician;

- taken clotting factor concentrates for a bleeding disorder such as hemophilia;

---

[7] Susan Sontag, *AIDS and its Metaphors.* (New York: Farrar, Straus and Giroux, 1989), 48. Landmarks occur in books.

- lived or was born in Cameroon, Central African Republic, Chad, Congo, Equatorial Guinea, Gabon, Niger, or Nigeria since 1977;

- taken drugs or money in exchange for sex since 1977;

- tested positive for HIV virus;

- had symptoms of HIV infection including unexplained weight loss, night sweats, blue or purple spots on or under the skin, long-lasting white spots or unusual sores in your mouth, lumps in your neck, armpits, or groin that last more than a month, fever higher than 99 degrees that lasts more than 10 days, diarrhea lasting over a month, or persistent cough and shortness of breath.[8]

I don't know anyone whose death resulted from AIDS. I have never even been The Friend when someone tests positive. These men belong to something, to each other, even. I do not. When I came out in college, and the guys

---

[8] These stipulations were Red Cross regulations as of October 6, 2002, when I accessed this list. It's worth noting that the Red Cross has loosened its country restrictions but as of 2010, "the Department of Health and Human Services Secretary's Advisory Committee on Blood Safety and Availability voted against recommending a change to the Food and Drug Administration (FDA) policy of a lifetime deferral for men who have sex with other men" (http:// www.redcrossblood.org, accessed January 25, 2016). Though I once had a job delivering for the Red Cross and understand blood shortages all too well, I cannot conscionably donate blood.

in my dorm posted a sign across from my door of two stick figures fucking that read *AIDES kills fags dead,* I was more upset at their misspelling than the implication that I had or would have AIDS. As an ex-anorexic, I was attracted to those neutered-but-fucking stick figures, staring at me, beckoning, incorporating me into one or both of them: self-portrait as the sex between them, bonded by demise.

7a.

I have never met Aunt Priscilla, but I imagine she never leaves her house without a cigarette and a Bible. She's not my aunt, but Wes's, who has posted his "Letter Wars" with Auntie Cilla on the internet. Basically, Wes writes letters to his family detailing his openly gay life and Priscilla takes issue with them. When the family reunion comes around, Cilla has an absolute hissy fit: "As soon as I found out you were planning to bring Tom, I told Susan *this creates a big problem* and that her and Dan should feel free to discontinue [...] the party. My opposition WAS AND STILL IS Tom being there."[9] Cilla objects on the grounds that Tom and Wes have an "unhealthy relationship and it is not

---

[9-13] The Letter Wars," last accessed June 10, 2002, http://www.officerwes.com/coolsite/ lttrindx.htm. Wes takes "Priscilla" from the name of a bus, christened by drag queens in *The Adventures of Priscilla, Queen of the Desert*. Besides an endless correspondence between aunt and nephew, the website also includes the not-to-be-missed catalog of "Things from Wes's Nose." Though Wes and Tom have now parted ways, Wes runs the site as an anti-homophobia resource page.

something I wish to expose my grandchildren, the other young children or even myself to."[10] I'm confused: does Tom don beige trench coats and flash old women at family barbecues? In a letter that must have made her hand ache, Aunt Priscilla writes:

> information from Oregon Health Department and the Center for Disease Control [makes] it . . . very apparent that the homosexuals and their communities run rampant with many exotic and common diseases. This does not only include HIV/AIDS … but T.B., syphilis, all types of veneral diseases, fungusses and Hepatitis A,B,C, & D. Hepatitis C & D are deadly and Hepatitis is much easier transmitted than some of the other diseases. The increase of Hepatitis in the State of Oregon has increased greatly with the influx of the homosexual population. We all know that just the slightest amount of fecal material is deadly so why in the world am I expected to put Tom before any of my grandchildren.[11]

Auntie Cill has done her homework. Apparently, she's not only afraid Tom and Wes will flash themselves but will also chuck fecal matter at family and guests. What's a cookout without a little dung flung amongst friends, I want to ask. The letter and its misspellings stretch on worse than a bar tab, ending with Priscilla insisting that she "truly believe[s] homosexuality is wrong, destructive and deadly…. I continue to love, care and pray for you."[12]

The letter wars become so heated that Cilla hires an attorney. I don't know Wes, but I imagine him chuckling as he reads an almost saccharine missive from Kenneth Magnum Esq., stating that Auntie Cill will sue if Wes publishes her full name or any of her "personally identifying information" and that Kenneth is "returning, unopened, this year's Christmas letters which you addressed to her and her husband and her son Butch. She has asked that you not initiate any further contact."[13] I'm not sure which I love more: the fact that Priscilla's son's name is Butch or that she is afraid of receiving calls from the people at Angry Homosexuals of America (AHA). My dream is Butch grows up to be a card-carrying member.

7b.

No one in my family comes close to the sheer hatred or distraught drunkenness of Aunt Priscilla. But, after my mother told her family about Dustin and me, questions involving our romantic lives dried up. One cousin thought we were doing it to be cool.[14] Another said to my mother: "I still love 'em, but they gotta know they can't act on it." His reaction characterized most of my Indiana relatives' response. *They can't act on it.*

My Indiana relatives are nice people. They live in Brownstown, which

---

[14] Receptive anal sex may be the most painful fashion trend since underwire or stilettos.

only has one stoplight.[15] I doubt any of them actually know homosexual people beyond Elton John and whatever diluted, dimensionally challenged versions NBC brings into their homes. On one visit, an uncle told my brother CJ, "You're so skinny I almost thought you had AIDS!" And that was the cool uncle. *AIDS and its Metaphors* has spread. I believed that the "illness flushes out an identity"; I wanted and feared to belong to the identity that, "among the risk group in the United States most severely affected in the beginning, homosexual men, [AIDS] has been a creator of community as well as an experience that isolates the ill and exposes them to harassment and persecution."[16] I wanted AIDS to belong to me. How sick am I?

8.

As of September 2, 2015, the cumulative number of AIDS cases reported to the Centers for Disease Control was 1,194,039. According to the CDC, "men who have sex with men (MSM) of all races and ethnicities remain the population most profoundly affected by HIV."[17]

---

[15] Until recently, it merely flashed yellow.

[16] Sontag, *AIDS and its Metapors*, 25. I want to add to this the "bugchaser parties" my friend Charlie went to. In these circles, Charlie reported, HIV *is part of the whole package of gay life.*

[17] "HIV in the United States: At a Glance," http://www.cdc.gov/hiv/statistics/overview/ataglance.html. One point two million is an incomprehensible number. It's not a way to remember the dead. Or a way to think about the living.

AIDS was originally called the "gay cancer," then spent a brief period under the marquee of Gay-Related Immune Deficiency.[18] "The gay community went absolutely nuts over that, and so they changed it to Acquired Immuno-deficiency Syndrome, and so AIDS was born in May of 1982," the writer of *The AIDS Epidemic in San Francisco: The Medical Response, 1981–1984, Volume I* says.[19] So, yes, "the gay community," who objected to commoner names like Tiffany, Thelonious, and GRID, "changed it" and thus "AIDS was born." I am a parent of AIDS.

I missed these first formative years, began really getting to know my AIDS as she was entering high school. By then, AIDS's belligerence had a death toll I only dreamed of when I myself was a Morrissey-listening angst-ridden anorexic mess who fantasized about the death of the guys in my speech class. I missed the protests where people would drop "dead" in the street, only to have their friends draw chalk outlines of them on sidewalks, on the concrete Earth, in order to illustrate the silence and death. I missed seeing, all over town, the bodies outlined in ghost white. I am the out-of-towner who comes the night of a sweeping thunderstorm: upon my arrival, even the out-lines of what has been recorded have nearly been erased.[20]

[18–19] http://sunsite.berkely.edu:2020/dynaweb/teiproj/oh/science/aids2@Generic_BookText-View369, last accessed April 10, 2002. The writer later disclaims links between AIDS and the gay community. But, at this moment, we own it. Flaunt it.

[20] I rely here on Judith Butler's recounting in an interview within *Radical Philosophy* 67 (Summer 1994). The text of this interview is available online, and worthy of your time, at http://www.theory.org.uk/but-int1.htm.

I'm angry at the erasure. I'm angry at a fellow poet, a lesbian, Georgia, who said one night, about Liz's HIV-positive friend Bernie, "Well, at least he can have unprotected sex as much as he likes now." I know I shouldn't take her ignorance for a sloughing off of custodial duties. But if AIDS isn't just a gay disease, if it doesn't belong to gay men or somehow situate them in the steam of identity, then why didn't Georgia know? The cheer in her voice searched for good fortune: "at least that's over with, now he's free to have *real* sex." Maybe I should let Georgia off the hook. In her defense, she also believed women urinate through the birth canal.

To excise AIDS from my body I need to erase Georgia's words that night. Erase from memory my friend Steven's high school health teacher who asks, "In what group did AIDS first appear and spread?" three times on the same twenty-five question test. I have erased most of the memory of the man who came to talk about being positive to Mrs. Bevilacqua's senior AP English class. I remember he looked healthy, but can't tell you if he was blond, clean-shaven, white. And I can't get rid of his nervous masculine voice and the first thing he said: "I am not a gay man. Any of you can get it."

9.

This essay is old—thirteen years have passed from the time it was first pub-lished. I read from it once in a bookstore to a bunch of fellow writers. Afterwards, a friend told me he heard someone near him lean over and ask a neighbor, "Why is this guy so proud to have AIDS?"

I have lived in a time when four letters arranged in distinct sequence meant a death sentence. What it means now is not that.

And yet. A good friend calls me to say two things: he is a methamphetamine addict. And he is HIV-positive. It is the positive diagnosis that makes him want to die. Makes him plan it.

Gay men on hookup sites now proclaim themselves "on PrEP," or pre-exposure prophylaxis, an antiretroviral drug which has proven highly effective to block transmission. The controversy has been substantial, but underneath is the desire to be sexually unfettered, unpoliced.

10.

End this.

I don't know how: there is no ending. I imagine AIDS like Freddy Kreuger from *Nightmare on Elm Street*. Targeting the too-young. Devouring their souls and bodies, ingesting, imprisoning them. I imagine the dead struggling inside of AIDS, stretching its skin, giving it heartburn.

When a friend recently seroconverted, I found myself making other metaphors: a rude houseguest that won't leave, who's fed a drug to make him or her as undetectable as possible, living small in the remotest parapets of the body. It isn't now the death knell it was when I was coming up. Now, a sleeping and dangerous beauty. Now, a manageable illness, less intrusive than diabetes.

AIDS has grown up, lost some of its teeth, matured, receded. Still, graffiti tells me "AIDS = Abstinence Is Definitely Smart." And online, I read somewhere "As I Die Slowly."

It's common for a queer person to feel as if he or she or they are "the only one." I always thought that AIDS might feel this way too. Alien, it creates a community of itself, a teeming, isolation-driven, loathing-loathed clan. I have to let go if I am to stop being colonized. Metaphors don't mean to colonize, but they do. If I do not relinquish AIDS, I will always be annexed by acronym, subjected to the surveillance of stethoscope and scales. I have to find new ways of dying, alive.

Be Destroyed

"CATS MUST GO TO GOOD HOME OR WILL BE DESTROYED," read the ad my father placed in the *Fort Lauderdale Pennysaver*. Our phone number followed.

"I want to know," the fifteenth woman that morning said between bursting sobs, "how you're going to kill those poor little animals!"

"They're going right into the wood chipper," I retorted, tired of fielding phone calls.

But his words worked. That day, my father said goodbye to a third of the 130 cats who had been living in our home. "Just let me be alone," he said to me at the end of it, closing the door, refusing to come out even to eat.

*

Enter our kitchen, and you'd see a ring of cats watching from above, perched and shedding sphinxes hunkered together in the hollowed-out caves where the soft lighting had been. The sentinel cats had pushed aside the frosted plastic shades and made themselves at home up there. Furry Rapunzels in self-exile, they let down hair and shat on the counters, on the stove, on top of the refrigerator and microwave. Turn on a stovetop burner and you would be greeted by the smell of singed cat hair. Or worse.

Some of them had free range. Others were caged in big coops made out of PVC pipe and chicken wire and carpet. Two cats per cage, two cages made a top and bottom bunk. Of course they were let out, for feeding time or when the cages were cleaned, which happened at least once every two days, depending on which of my two brothers was on duty that week. One of the rooms in the house was emptied of its professional office furniture (a sprawling desk with a maze of cherrywood cabinets, a computer and attached printer, all the business files from CJ's Courier Service, Inc., the radio equipment, the five-line telephones: all evacuated to make room). It was the cat room: a carpet of newspapers cleared three times a day and relaid, and edged around the room were the cat boxes, like one continuous gray-pebble baseboard.

By the end, when my father placed the newspaper ad, the cages also lined our back screened-in porch, out by the kidney-shaped pool whose motor choked on kitty litter. By the end, there were 131 of them, some rescues, others born in—there is no other way to say it—captivity.

By the end, I mean of my parents' marriage.

My parents met in Indiana, in a factory that fashioned sonobuoys, military devices used to detect submarine radar signals.

My mother approached my father: You look familiar, from high school? But my father had finished high school 911 miles away.

For their first date, my father flew her to that sleepy town in Florida. He drove her to Daytona Beach, where he wooed her at a club at the water's edge, swaying to music that spilled out on the deck, where they took breaks from dancing to lean out over the ocean. It must have seemed to her that it could always be this romantic—hot jazz rippling over the endless silky Atlantic.

At the end of the trip, after he'd introduced her to his parents, my father's mother said, "I guess you want the ring you gave to that other girl now?"

My father proposed at the plant. I think of them there: my father in slacks, my mother draped in painting clothes, a breathing mask over her mouth. I want to go back now. I want to keep my mother's mouth obscured, obstructed, I want to stop him from bending to his knee, I want to protect him from her *yes*.

*

CJ's Courier Service was my parents' brainchild; they started it with the sole purpose of giving my older brother something to do after he graduated high school. It was named after him because he was supposed to run it, after it took off. The first client was my uncle Terry's toxicology lab in Hialeah. CJ was the first driver and my parents ran the business out of our five-bedroom ranch-style house in Weston, Florida, a modestly affluent section in the westernmost part of what was then unincorporated Fort Lauderdale. We lived on Westwood Lane, on a cul-de-sac where, our realtor informed us, Anthony Quinn had owned the large house three doors down. The front yard was home to rock gardens, a boasting palm tree, bushes of Mexican heathers under the windows, and in the back was a baby banana tree. Maybe because of the proximity to the pool and its chlorine, maybe because our dog Rocky marked it constantly with his piss, maybe because of bad dumb luck, who knows, the tree never bore any fruit. It never thrived, but it held on.

Within two years we had acquired major accounts, employees answering phones and processing payroll, and a cadre of drivers who used their own cars to make deliveries for customers such as Owens & Minor and the Red Cross. Drivers we equipped with long-range radios, drivers zipping through the streets of Miami-Dade and Broward County all day, every day of the year. Even Christmas. Someone always answered the phone in the middle of the night at our house. At our house the ringer was never off. For someone, there was never a full night's rest, never peace.

My parents built a life around emergency rooms and patients bleeding on a table and babies born to crack mothers who needed their first shits tested immediately so doctors would know how to treat these tiniest of addicts. My parents built a life around the word *stat*. Around speed and need. They built the kind of life that cannot last.

Sometimes I wished we could train the cats to answer the phones, dispatch calls, answer customer complaints, complete billing requests, follow up on unpaid invoices, reboot the servers. At least clean the desks, shred the mountains of old delivery sheets, pay the drivers. Vacuum the fucking floors.

*

"Your mother started seeing a man in Daytona Beach, when she was cleaning condos out there. He was a doctor, I found his card in her purse. You were three. That was the first time." My father doesn't say what he was doing rifling through my mother's purse, and I don't ask. I am twenty-four years old; he is a fifty-four-year-old man who is trying to stop his shattered-windshield life from breaking beyond repair. We are in my bedroom, talking. My mother is thinking about leaving him again and that has made me my father's two a.m. confidante.

There were more, he says. Passionate men, pockets full of money and promises. More moonlight on the ocean. When those faded, my father swept in from stage left, the Consoler, the Absolver, eager to take her back.

When I was twelve, a police officer started coming to the house to collect her at night. I don't remember him except as a large shape filling the front door's open gap, right hip with its holstered gun, left hip against the jam as he waited for her to emerge, my cinnamon-scented mother, criminal in her red silk blouse. The trail of her nearly crackled as she left through the front door.

One night my father says he went looking for them. He tucked my mother's gun in his slacks. He was on foot, approaching the squad car parked in the empty church parking lot. The car shook on its shocks, the windows fogged over. My father tells me he drew the weapon, clicked the safety off.

I'm telling you this so you know: My father had a choice. And he always chose my mother.

*

We delivered anything.

Once, a client's dog when he was called suddenly out of town and needed the drooling, benevolent St. Bernard taken to his father's in South Miami.

Once, a very expensive cellular telephone to a man named Martin P. Straight.

Once, a big R2-D2-shaped container filled with dry ice and stem cells (when opened, the fog drifted over the top of it, like a witch's cauldron), which would then be re-infused into a cancer patient's body.

Once, a dildo.

Actually, twice, accompanied with women's underwear and high heel shoes.

Once, a voice on the other end of the phone telling me to turn around, the blood wasn't needed, the patient had died on the table. Once upon a time, hurry. We were saviors.

*

The cats lived on two acres of open field behind a six-office strip mall at the end of Broward Boulevard in Sunrise. On the south side, the strip mall was bordered by a canal that ran parallel to State Road 84, the feeder for Interstate 595. To the west, a trailer park. On the north, a church that owned the field but had neither cleared nor developed it yet. The cats came most likely from the trailer parkers, who abandoned their animals to the field whenever they moved, or a hurricane threatened. Which meant every summer, since this was Fort Lauderdale at the beginning of global warming.

CJ's Courier Service took up a cavernous three-room office in the strip mall, which also housed a 7-Eleven, a Domino's Pizza, a Chinese takeout joint, and a space rented to a Korean religious group that held services very late at night. The cats begged for scraps outside the front door of Domino's, and at the back door of the Chinese delivery, scarfing up the fried rice and dried-out pepperoni slices no one ordered. They flooded the dumpsters looking for food and shelter. Despite getting used to years of human neglect, they let us approach, they lowered their heads, they deigned to be touched gently.

*

The most omnipresent of the cats was Boots, cursed with a constant running nose and a need for attention. When I remember him now, pacing hungrily from Domino's to Chinese to the 7-Eleven, his running nose investigating the edibility of all discarded trash, wandering too close to the road, not paying attention, too close to his own desires to realize he could be killed, I understand how impossible it was to ignore the impulse to save him—him and his purring, mangy ilk. Poor, sweet Boots, who was not promised a next meal or a bath, who once nosed a Snickers wrapper so hard that it was glued with his snot to his fur.

*

The steamrollers came on a Monday morning. Mist still hung above the field.

I was alone in the office and when I opened the back door to see what the commotion was, there they were in the backfield, like tractors but with glinting rollers that flattened the field's scrub brush. My mother was there within fifteen minutes. Without her face on, waving at the rollers to stop, blocking them with her thin body, arguing with the men who got down off their deathtraps, her speech so fiery I could see speckles of spit flying out. She was joined by Sue, the cat lady who had begun to feed the cats originally, the woman who kept them from going hungry. But they couldn't stop every bulldozer. The most my mother and Sue could do was dig into the big mounds of dirt that had filled with mewling. The most they could save was thirty cats from being buried alive.

*

The first day, they were on the five o'clock and eleven o'clock news. Close-up of the cutest and youngest ones, an armful of them wriggling and mewling. Then our phone number flashed and well-meaning citizens came to adopt cats that were not anyone's vision of cuddly—cats that were, in fact, in need of medical attention and, in Boots's case, nasal surgery. Imagine the soccer mom coming to adopt a kitten for her second-grade daughter and meeting instead a hissing, near-feral feline, and you'll see begin to understand the difficulty. The trouble was she couldn't love what she didn't want to hold.

And before we knew it, they multiplied.

*

Boots, Feets, Mouth, Legs.

Brute, Mama Bear.

Little Miss Gray Kitty and Big Mister Gray Kitty. Orange Guy. Tri Guy.

Names like bus drivers': Gus. Tommy. Harry. Sebastian. Sylvester Jr.

Label names. Meanness. Grandma. Rainbow.

Diamond, who died as a kitten. My brother Dustin buried him in the backyard before my mother could find him gone.

The last one to live with us: Strawberry, née Strawbaby, named for her reddish fur, though my mother called her Straw. "As in, The Last," she said.

The last known dead: Socks, a gray scruffy cat who in his old age would make this screeching battle cry to say, "Carry me to a cat box *now*, if you know what's good for you," but who could not always wait.

Buddy and Midnight. When Midnight fell sick and wouldn't move off his little piece of carpet, we were sure he was going to die. Buddy nosed his bowl over by his friend's barely breathing side. They lay there, two cats against the world. Midnight recovered. Love can do that to an animal.

There were 131, and they all had names; my father memorized each one. They were all little allegories: lost innocents, last chances, neglected signs. They lived with us and we fed them, and we became the crazy cat house, served with legal papers filed by the homeowner's association, all those notices that went ignored.

They multiplied, and my mother became a kind of feline night-nurse, first delivering litters of kittens, then seeing to the runts, caring for the sick, the ones that would not take their mother's milk. My mother would hold these kittens in her arms and feed them from a bottle. She learned to first drape them in a towel, folded and tucked carefully at the neck, so that they would not scratch and bite her. She sang to them. She named them.

It is a law of human nature: anything you name, you own. The converse is also true: what you name owns you back. This is how it is to be loved; also, destroyed.

*

The cat love was like an infection in my family. First, it was CJ who took to them, helping Sue the Cat Lady feed them at night. Sue was pretty, with long blonde hair down to her narrow waist, and bright blue eyes that looked, but weren't in fact, cross-eyed. She was quick to tell CJ that her husband was a cop, and that he wouldn't allow her any more animals in their nearby trailer. She already had two cats, a dog, and a potbellied pig.

I started calling CJ Dances With Cats, much to my mother's amusement and then it was she who befriended Sue: two blond ladies out at sunset, laying down plastic plates of cat food, talking through the feeding hour, friends united in saving their little corner of the world.

Finally it was my father, maybe around the sixty-cat mark, around the time that the collection of cats became unmanageable for everyone else. My father, saying, "If you can get rid of them then what kind of person are you? They're innocent in all of this." And, "I'm not asking you to help me, I can take care of them all by myself." Knowing he couldn't possibly work two jobs and wash thirty cat boxes every day. Knowing full well. But blind to it, like a man in love, like a man who needed something to save and protect, something that would need him back.

*

My father was fired from the toxicology lab where he worked. By his brother.

Then CJ's Courier Service lost our largest three clients, laid off its drivers, and struggled to make the bills.

The collectors began circling like vultures, calling at all hours of the business day, asking for my parents, who we were told never to say were home. Once, when the Bank of America called asking for Marsha Hall, my mother said into the phone, "I'm not in right now."

The collector left a message.

*

One afternoon, I entered my older brother's bedroom to wake him for his shift at the courier service. He manned the night shift and it started a little earlier on Thursdays because Dustin and I codirected a gay and lesbian youth group that met those nights. This particular day, CJ was pissed at me because I had just returned from "vacation." The vacation was the last of the five trips required to complete my low-residency master of fine arts degree in poetry at Bennington College in Vermont; each of those ten days was filled with lectures and readings, workshops and seminars. I called it invigorating or draining, but never a vacation.

CJ refused to get out of bed, telling me, "I don't care if you miss your fucking gay group." I started pulling off the blankets, tugging away even his pillows from his waterbed. The cat that stayed in his room hid in his closet. One of the pillows landed in her rarely changed litter box. CJ stood up and drew back a clenched fist. I put my arms up, Evander Holyfield-style, protecting my face. My ears began to ring. I pushed into him, knocking him back into the bed. I picked up his box fan and threw it at his body, which was already rising from the bed. Another round of fists on me. My mother flung open the door to his room, saw my older brother wailing on me, and tackled him to the bed. That's when I picked up the cat box and threw its muddy contents on my shirtless brother, splashing him all over his chest with cat shit. Then I ran to my room, moved my desk in front of the door, sat there trying to catch my breath, holding tissue to the bleeding parts of my face.

"You guys have to cool it," my father scolded us. "You can't bother your mother with any of this. She can't handle it." The law became: don't knock on her door, don't let her answer the phone, even if you're in the bathroom. Protect her at all costs.

What she couldn't handle: not just the petty fights, moving out of the strip mall office in the middle of the night, leaving no forwarding address, becoming defendants in a lawsuit for breach of contract.

She couldn't handle laying off all the drivers—Amy and Richard and their sixty-year-old mother; Earl with his gnarly tattoos and his gay biker bar stories; eighty-year-old Abe who brought us a bag of bagels once a month. The drivers were like family and they kept calling, wanting to know when they could expect to be paid. The only difference between our former employees and our present collectors was the pleading tone.

My mother stayed locked behind her door, parked at our only remaining computer all day, logged into Yahoo chatrooms that centered on, at first, psychic readers and, later, on swinging singles.

"Leave her alone," he said, squeezing my shoulder tight.

*

One night, at the dinner table, my mother and I sat across from each other, spinning spaghetti around our silent forks. We were the only people home;

everyone else still out delivering. She wore her blue silk bathrobe, her hair unwashed, uncombed. She looked like a woman who had fought too long.

It was the hour in South Florida where everything went red, the palm trees, the mock-adobe houses, the sprinklers coming on, their shots of stuttering water, the cars coughing on the congested highways, everything bathed in a surrendering sun.

She thanked me for dinner then asked how things were going. "Fine," I said, meaning *traitor.*

"Good," she said, meaning *please let there be some part of you who still loves his mother.*

Behind us 131 cats were waiting for my father to come home and feed them. I could hear them breathing.

*

In those days, my mother was always on the phone with another man and my father was locked out of the bedroom. He slept in my room, in a chair with his feet up on my bed, dismissing me when I insisted he lie down. "It's just for a few hours, Jame." I found him, mornings, in the rooms of that house, laying on the area rugs, his body unblanketed, his shirt rolled up underneath his head. More than once, he risked the stench of the living room, where the cats lived. There he'd be, among them, on the leather couch, sleeping sitting up, a pile of cats in his lap and on either side of him, asleep too.

*

The day she left my father for Mr. Panties, I woke early and dressed quickly in the dark. I wanted to be gone. I wrote a note and slipped it into one of her boxes, then drove to a friend's house nearby.

My father drove her to the man's hotel; my mother drove the man's car back to our house. My father loaded her boxes into his car with my brothers' help.

At the last minute, she took a cat with her too, the gray one with the white paws named Socks, who was born a hermaphrodite.

*

When my mother left, my father moved back into his room. He began not sleeping in his own bed.

Then he was the furtive one, trying to displace the other man.

One late night as he was talking to my mother on the phone, a policeman came to arrest my father. He'd delivered a mobile phone downtown and parked illegally, blocking a hydrant. A judge had signed the warrant; the cop showed it to me when I answered the door. "Larry Hall," he said gruffly, his voice official and trying not to choke on the animal smell. He shifted his weight back and forth between his legs, pulling down at his vest as he waited. He was a young guy; the uniform still looked like a costume.

I convinced him to let my father put on a shirt, I convinced him not to use the handcuffs. I saw my father duck into the squad car, and I cursed him. He'd borrowed money from my grandmother to buy twenty-six dozen roses—one dozen for each year of their marriage—and sent them to my mother. Instead of paying off the parking ticket.

*

The note I left in one of my mother's boxes—the pots and pans—read, "I've been watching you leave for months. I just couldn't watch anymore."

*

About a third of the cats were adopted by people who answered the ad.

Another third of the cats my father deposited at my grandmother's house in rural Homestead. She sometimes called with updates about the cats, and after those talks, my father would cry.

The last third my father took back to the field at the end of Broward Boulevard. That empty field which had been plowed and leveled, flattened, had actually never been developed, never not an empty field where abandoned cats went to find shelter. It is hard to picture my father, loading up the cats he loved—the ones with their claws still, the ones he said still possessed what he called "a fighting chance"—but it's even harder for me to picture him unloading them into the world and leaving them there to fend for themselves.

My father was so good at loving things.

He never learned how to stop doing it intensely, believing if he loved something hard enough it wouldn't fail him again.

IN LIEU OF DRUGS

Your brother wakes up in a hospital. An IV curls away from his arm. It is either Wednesday night or Thursday morning. He is strapped down while the nurse at the desk chats up a police officer. The cop says he's never seen such a *hardcore user*, and the nurse says she's never administered such heavy rehydration. Their tone is not shocked, it is jovial. He exists somewhere between night and morning, dark and light, nameless: the patient, the criminal, the user, the used. He is one of 103,000 crystal-related emergency room visits in 2011, one of the numberless addicts in America. He is not your brother; he is *just another meth-head dying for a fix*. He is discharged in the morning by a nurse who turns her nameless back while he dresses, then wheels him to the curb and packs him into a waiting taxi. He thanks her, calling her ma'am.

*

My brother tells me he is an addict over the telephone on April Fools' Day,

2011. "Dustin, that's not very funny," I say, and he begins to cry. My brother hadn't even been drunk until he turned twenty-seven. Never smoked anything a day in his life. So I can't be blamed that it takes some convincing that my brother, *straight-edge* all his life, has become a terrific meth addict.

After he's convinced me, after he's told me everything, I am driving to a friend's house, I am in her doorway, in her arms. It's her idea: *you should go to Pittsburgh*, she says, *I'll drive you down to Syracuse*, meaning the closest airport, three hours away. She says, *I'm sorry I'm not crying with you, but my Valium kicked in just before you got here. Do you want one?*

*

When he opens the door to his apartment his face crumples with emotion. Over his shoulder, I see the dirty dishes towering precariously on the modest dinette, on the glass coffee table, on the slender bookshelves near the kitchen. In the living room, cat feces. It would be inaccurate to say "piles" since the cat is old and incontinent. He defecates in streak-mounds. The dishes in the sink—plain white Ikea bowls and plates—are caked with macaroni gone gold-en-brown, unfinished tuna fish sandwiches hard as cement, oatmeals and rices desiccated at the water line. I remember when Dustin bought those dishes, the first he ever picked out. I called them boring but he smiled and said, *Classic.*

While he is at work, I clean out the fridge, throwing away mostly empty jars of salsa, leftovers gone bad, a carton of sour milk. I scrub a sticky brown substance from one of the drawers. I wash the dishes. I cringe at the internet history on his computer. I google Narcotics Anonymous and Outpatient Rehabilitation. I leave messages on machines. One woman calls back the next day, tentative-voiced. I say, "My brother told me he was an addict," and she says, "It's better if he calls himself," but still gives me an intake appointment for next week.

"Nothing this week?" I question in that insistent way I have that tries to be polite.

"Nothing this week," she confirms, her voice a little sad. I probably sound desperate. My plane leaves on Sunday. Dustin needed to be comfortably saved by Saturday.

At night, we watch TV and eat dinner together, sitting on the couch, talking until midnight, blankets and pillows piled around us like it's a slumber party. He laughs at all the same jokes we like to make, we tell the familiar family stories. We stay on recognizable ground. It feels good to be first person pluraled: we are not torn, we are not lost.

He was at a party, someone's house in Pittsburgh. Men he knew retreated to a back bedroom, and he followed them, saw them light a pipe. *It's not for you, pretty boy,* they laughed, when he asked what it was. The laugh stung. When they left, Dustin took up the lighter, he lay flame to the pipe's bed, my brother's first time getting high. And was still high, a little, the next day when he picked me up from the Pittsburgh airport.

I'd taken a taxi, two buses, and two airplanes to arrive in Pittsburgh, so that we could cross the rest of Pennsylvania, the sliver of West Virginia, the yawn of Ohio, all the way to southeast Indiana, where my grandmother lie in a hospital bed, the thin flicker of her life wavering, her lungs inhaling whatever breath the machines gave her ungrateful body. He drove the whole way, insisting he was more alert. We'd gotten the same text message from CJ: *Grandma had a stroke last night. In hospital now. Don't call. Going to sleep.*

We saw her body on Monday morning, in the first minutes of ICU visiting hours. *She's not her body anymore,* I thought as Dustin commenced reading her the sports page in his cheery newscaster voice. He could have been an anchor with his ready-for-TV good looks, his dark hair swept back, his face tan even in October. There was a story about a basketball player from the Miami Heat, whose games she attended. If Grandma Hall didn't wake up to hear Heat news, she was truly gone. I didn't know then how intent my brother was on following her to the cliffs, into the coal-shimmering beyond.

*

I will want to know who tied his bicep, who injected him. How frequently he used. How the needle felt, piercing the vein. I'll want to be inside the story, to travel along its arterial arcs.

I'll wonder what he looked like the night—a Wednesday—he was found wandering the swanky hotel's hallway, hiding by the vending machines and the fake plastic trees, thinking himself invisible, a ninja, the dealer gone— packed up and fled, telling him, *You talk too much.* This is how my little brother showed up in the hotel clerk's story of that night: *some deranged tweaker, muscle- bound druggie, we called the cops.*

There will never be enough details to comfort me, leave me sated.

*

One Saturday morning in late April, I wake to a series of strange text messages from my brother. When I message him and ask, "What is this all about?" his reply describes an unsafe sexual practice, lists an address in downtown Pitts- burgh. I call him and he answers, a blurry diminished voice saying *Just a joke, I have to go now.*

I have papers to grade, but I can't stop leaving messages, my tone alternately disbelieving, angry, recriminating, sorrowful. I think, *Screw the papers, get in your car, drive.* But I know, with increasing disgust, that I can't protect him where he's gone. I can drive the nine hours to Pittsburgh, but who knows where he'll be, what good I'll do. I turn back to the papers, pen in hand. While I am correcting halfheartedly someone's halfhearted grammar, the cops raid the club.

I am so glad to hear his voice when he calls, hours later, I forgive him almost instantly. I listen to the story he tells of the raid, how one of the workers kept him hidden, ushering him from room to room, a bathhouse refugee. I don't think to ask until later: why would an underpaid clerk risk jail time for a junkie? And then the answer swims in to the vein of understanding: my brother was delusional, the clerk was taking advantage of him, having some mean fun.

*

While You're Using

1. Drink lots of water. Crystal meth dehydrates you.

2. If you're snorting, have your own straw or bumper. After, squirt saline spray or snort warm water up each nostril.

3. If you're slamming, use alcohol swabs and fresh cotton to clean a spot before you hit. This will help you avoid abscesses.

4. Sugar may be tempting but if you've got an appetite while using, eat protein and complex carbs. Did somebody order a burrito with whole wheat tortilla?

5. Tuna fish is loaded with protein, tyrosine, tryptophan and other stuff to restore a weary tweaker. Plus there are no dishes to wash off if you eat it from the can!

6. Tell your regular using friends what your limits are and stay firm to your goal, even if they make jokes or try to "tempt" you otherwise.

7. Establish a "purchase limit" with your dealer. Yes, some dealers WILL do this to keep you a stable and sane customer!

Mid-May, on a road trip with friends to New Orleans and Houston, relapse. Walking Houston Shirtless and Disoriented Relapse. Sunburned Relapse. People Shouting Out Their Car Windows at the Crazy Man in Traffic Relapse. Lying to His Friends Relapse. Friday Night Saturday All Damn Weekend Long If I Want to Rage I Can Sleep on Sunday Relapse. Relapse. Relapse.

*

List of Delusions (Addict's)

1. Someone is following him, he says, hushed into the phone, from one of the laundry rooms in his apartment building. He won't say which one. "They're *listening*. They sent dogs into the building to find me." He hides in various laundry rooms on each floor of his apartment building, trying to throw them off his trail. This is the day I've been dreading: the day he gets busted. They've bugged his cell phone. "Hold on," his panic commands. Then static. Then, "No no no," and the line goes dead. Repeat for two hours.

2. The police have mounted a searchlight on the apartment building opposite my brother's. They are shining into his apartment, tracking him; he must crouch down when he moves in front of the windows.

3. One night, the police break down his door, find him in his bedroom, only in underwear. One officer tells him to stand, kicks his legs farther apart, says, *Hands flat on the wall*. He stays that way until he can't feel his feet, his hands are

freezing, he is shaking from numbness. When he finally gets the nerve to break the position, he finds his apartment door lightly ajar. The cat, curled in a ball by the door, has slept through everything.

4. Downstairs in the basement at a sex party, my brother is shooting up with another guy. Porn plays on the television. When the drug takes effect, my brother begins narrating the porn, which he sees as a black and white home movie. He is the grandmother character, the voiceover of some of our most cherished childhood memories. "Can you," says his friend-in-crystal, "just shut the fuck up?" My brother sniffs and clutches for his pearls. "That's no way to talk to your grandmother, young man."

*

I move to his one-bedroom cat-cramped apartment in June, after the semester's close, to help him get sober. *Think of me as your roommate,* I say, and he agrees, adding, *You are not the police.* June is a "trial month."

While he's at work, I put my head under the bed, slide fingers between couch cushions. I look in the tea kettle, in the freezer. Make a sweep of the cupboards. Search the pillowcases. Turn inside out the drawers of tchotchkes. Peer into the abyss of the storage closet, a disaster of discarded boxes. Feel my energy flag, dashed on the jagged rocks of all that clutter. *If he's that desperate to stash it in there, then he can have it.* I fasten a piece of tape above the door to see if he'll open it. Nothing makes me more scared than my brother finding out I'm a spy. Because I want this to be a story I can tell, I cannot be trusted.

When he gets home from work, I check the gym bag for needles or baggies while he is in the shower. I'm back at the computer when the water switches off, ready to greet him cheerily. *How was your day?*

*

Trial: 1. A judicial examination 2. A mode of testing qualities.

Exhibit A: Kit is leaning over my seat, whispering, "Who's going to drop some Ecstasy with me?" Kit is Dustin's friend, a muscle-bound massage therapist whose wife, Mallory, is sitting behind Dustin. We are on a yellow school bus with thirty other perfect strangers who bought tickets to the Pittsburgh Pride Pub Crawl, an annual event that rents out buses and keeps them running to the gay bars and clubs in the Emerald City's various neighborhoods. Kit wraps his arms around my brother's shoulders. His biceps bulge beneath his shirt. His beer breath smells sweet. Dustin and I hesitate. I think: *Alcohol isn't meth. Ecstasy isn't meth.* In the hesitation, my brother says no.

Exhibit B: Somewhere in the middle of the bar tour, I remember this kid getting on the bus, bombed beyond belief. I am my usual gregarious drunk self, making friends, getting the bus into a sing-along of Madonna tunes. The boy, a thin waif in a ripped t-shirt and dirty jeans and bright blue Converse, refuses to join in on "Like a Prayer." He eyes me intently though he can't keep focus. In a lull between tracks, he raises his voice and tells me with a half-grin, "I am going to break a bottle over your fucking head." Then he squeals. I shut up, and my brother sits beside me, putting himself between me and my new nemesis.

Exhibit C: After the bus tour ends, I am waiting on a street, three a.m., in dirty humid downtown Pittsburgh. I refuse to sit on the sidewalk, though I have been waiting for almost an hour, sending texts to Kit and Mallory and Dustin inside the nameless after-hours club. I was refused entrance, a fact they're ignorant of, and I am rolling cigarette after cigarette, talking to passersby. This is not my city. Then my brother appears, saying, "Wait here," and flips open his phone, walking as if searching for a signal, disappearing around a corner, the last time I see my brother on the night that refuses to end.

Exhibit D: I'm on Kit's couch, Mallory's spare quilt covering me, when my brother's phone pocket-dials me. He is muffled through his jeans, voice filtered down to its modulating vowels. I can hear another voice, distant but gruff. It's like they are draped in layers of gauze. Mummified. I have to keep listening. I am the witness, collecting evidence, the handwriting expert, discerning codes that might return my brother to me.

Exhibit E: *Dustin*, I hiss, trying not to alert Kit and Mallory, upstairs sleeping. *Dustin*, again, testing the limits of the whisper. Until finally, my voice burrows up from the pocket, he hears me and digs my voice free. "Jamie, what are you doing," he says, blurred, slowed down. He says my name again, then *don't, what, no, it's fine.*

128

When Dustin does come to collect me, the sun is just breaking, he's wearing yesterday's clothes, his hair is a mess. In the car home, he says I've ruined his good time—the man hurried out on him because he'd thought my brother was cop-wired. He could have been hurt. I keep repeating, my voice straining for control: "You left me. On a street. In Pittsburgh." We stare at each other, brothers who'd grown up fast, without protection. We are ascending one of those steep hills in god-knows-what-neighborhood of a dying city. He breaks the stare and swerves the wheel, saying he should just end it. I cry out his name, sharply, and he rights the car. We sit in silence in that too-early light that burns the back of the eyeballs.

Exhibit F: In that blaring morning light, I know that he is going to die.

Exhibit G: And that he is going to make me watch.

*

List of Delusions (Author's)

1. At some point this story will come to an end, as time has an end.

2. At some point the human spirit cannot endure more pain.

3. I can stop him.

4. I can save him.

5. I am powerful, he is powerless. I have the health this diseased man needs. We are each other's opposite, we are twins.

*

I take my brother to his first Narcotics Anonymous meeting in June. He doesn't go back to that meeting—Rainbow Bridge, they call themselves—until August. In between those months is July, a wide chasm that contains a story I can not tell you, his *rock bottom*:

I am teaching in Iowa City for three weeks. Between my brother and me stretches 670 miles, a   /   that terrifies me, but probably makes him feel free. He says he isn't   /   but it's a lie. A lie is white noise, a code that   /   what can't be said, a row of blank letters   /   waiting to be filled in. *I won't do it again, I won't lie,* he says,   /   but it's only code   /   *One day I'll disappear, I'll be the   /   in the story you need me to be,   /   I'll graduate past all your words.* It is code   /   I can't hear.

Then one night comes, he   /   . I can't reach him,   /   the phone is dead.   /   All night   /   //   //   /   . I can't sleep.   //   I read   /   my students' essays again   /   and again, thankful / for the white spaces   /   margins   /   where I write   /   my questions. My breathing   //   // makes a deal   /   with silence.

Later, he tells me he spent that night at   /   's, and what I imagined (rubber bands on biceps, men passed out on hardwood floors) comes rushing back to fill up the silence. But maybe that was just my imagination telling the story. How do you trust an imagination's rendering of your brother, high and   /   ? How does a mind make   /   into sense? Do the white spaces add

130

and add   /   until the page breaks? Isn't the imagination invested in making absence   /   account for itself?   //   Let me practice that chemistry in the blanks   /   Let me write a series of sentences that do not end   /   July is a story filled in with a question mark   /   I'm sure memory says   /   I'm not says the imagination   /   meanwhile the spaces go on   / adding   /   what   /   to now

*

I know that I will have to let you make up your own mind about my brother.
I know that if you do not treat him kindly, I will hurt you.

*

The story turns in August: daily meetings, nightly talks with his sponsor, the end. But I know an ending is just two words slapped onto something to give it shape.

*

From *The Twelve Traditions of Narcotics Anonymous:*
Recovery has to be learned and doesn't come easily.
This may be the essence of our insanity, not believing our own witness.

*

One August morning, I wake to the neighbor pounding on our door, her eyes red-rimmed at nine a.m. "Are you all right, Pat?" She is in her eighties and shaking a little; her silver bob looks like it could use a comb.

"Do you have a bottle of beer?" she asks.

"You couldn't have come to a worse place." I make my tone both apologetic and firm. I notice the wrinkles in the clothes she's slept in.

"Maybe in the way back of the fridge? Dustin looks like he'd keep a bottle back there, nice and cold." She's grasping the doorjamb. "I just need a bottle of beer," she says, then fixes herself a little taller. "Well, I don't *need* it, you understand. I just *want* it."

"I'm sorry, Pat."

"Right. Well, can you *drive* me to the liquor store?"

"I don't have a car, Pat. Can I call someone for you?"

"No, that's all right. Thanks anyhow."

Through the closed door, I can hear her knocking on the next neighbor's door. When he answers it, Pat informs him, "Dustin's brother said you'd take me to the liquor store."

When I tell him this story later, Dustin says, "That girl needs a program to work," which is NA speak for *Get your life together*. He tells me about the time Pat forgot the potatoes boiling on the stove and passed out on her couch. Dustin smelled smoke, found her door ajar, and knocked the blackened pot off its burner. When the firemen came and asked what happened, Pat looked wryly at them and said, "Oh, nothing. I just nearly burned us all up!"

At the end of August, when I'm leaving Pittsburgh, I run into the maintenance guy who tells me that Pat died in her apartment just a few weeks after. It is a story I do not tell my brother. I am not sure he can bear it.

*

Christmas Eve, 2011, the temperature at zero, an Indiana winter wind scratching at the cartilage in my ears. We've come to visit family but have left early to catch an NA meeting in Columbus, the town where we were born. When it's my turn, I rise, I say the words, "My name is Jamie, and I'm an addict." It's a closed meeting, but too cold outside: I've made my choice. I've spent so long seeing my brother as different—across a divide, challenging the edges of himself—for once it feels good to acknowledge there is no hierarchy separating us. We are brothers, addicts. What else is a story but memory in recovery?

Because it's Christmas Eve, people have brought potluck: there's a crock-pot of little sausages in a barbecue sauce, two baked chickens, potato salad, soda and desserts galore. We eat happily, while people share: telling the stories in order to wake themselves from narrative's thrall.

At the end of the meeting, while I'm carefully but ignorantly rolling a fresh cigarette among the addicts, my brother asks a woman how he can help clean up. She says, *Take some of this food home, we got a mess of cake.* He emerges with a whole sheet of Boston cream pie.

The next day is spent with our friends Julie and Angie. I have not told anyone about Dustin's addiction (why don't I say his *recovery*?), and so I try not to wince when our friends order margaritas at the Mexican restaurant. I try not to envy them their tequila, which comes in handy when they meet our family. Later, we are back at the hotel, and suddenly hungry, when Dustin remembers the cake. He retrieves it, serves it on a paper plate, perching four plastic forks at right angles.

"But where did this come from?" Julie asks. The question hangs in the room. Dustin clears his throat as he tells our friends his story. I listen, relieved to be returned to mere audience member. When he reaches the end, Julie cocks her head to one side, her eyes widening. "So this cake is in lieu of drugs?" My breath catches; I wait for my brother's laugh. When it comes, it calls for mine. Then all four of us are laughing so hard, we are crying. We have each other to hold on to.

I Liked You Better Before I Knew You So Well

"Your smile melts me," M. says, from his side of the bed. The windows are open, unblinded to a New York City evening in sweltering May, the heat rising from the concrete, surging through the unscreened windows, lodging in our bodies. Even the chardonnay we'd had at dinner needed an ice cube halfway through. Now we are in his bedroom, undressing with the lights on.

"I bet you hear that all the time, you little slut."

I laugh. "I can count the number of guys I've had sex with on one hand and still have fingers left over. This one," I say, raising my middle finger.

"You are a saucy boy." The blue in his eyes twinkles. "Someone should teach you a lesson."

*

He did not rape me that night.

This is not what I came here to tell you.

I've driven from Pittsburgh to New York City to meet M., excited about a man for the first time since Brandon and I broke up. M. has just moved from upstate New York back to the city to take a new job. When I'd asked what it was, he'd only allow, "I do research." His pictureless online profile location listed New Jersey. He'd sent me shirtless photos over email but would not reveal a last name. "I'll tell you when we meet." Before we met, I'd pore over the pictures which revealed a muscular body, fit in the way that almost hurts to hug. I nearly memorized the online notes in which he detailed his passions: classical music, contemporary poetry, sex.

This is our first date. We are in his bedroom after dinner. The supple sweep of his chest as it stretches and then flexes back to rest makes my mouth go dry. He watches me, too, and when I blush under the gaze, and smile at his appreciation, he encourages me with that line: *Your smile melts me.* He is what I want in a man: sincerity and lust and athletic musculature. Someone I can melt. *You little slut.*

*

"My dick is hardwired for fucking," he writes in an email before we meet. "If you want to come, you should do it while I'm fucking you. After I come, I usually want to go to sleep."

What am I that this excites me? Excites me in a way I can't name,

136

and almost as much as the snippet of a Breyten Breytenbach quote that follows as his signature line: "Exiled memory is the slow art of forgetting the color of fire." Be still my stupid heart.

*

A man who loves poetry. A man who knows exile and coldness correlate directly. This is the man who would rape me.

But not yet.

His bed: best night's sleep I've ever had.

I remember the sunrise in the morning, the way the light gave his body back to the world.

*

One theory holds that names contain their descriptors: the name is always inside, waiting to bloom up from its seed, to be extracted from its deep essence.

Another theory: names are imposed, and once the name settles on a thing, it cuts away, occludes other possibilities. Name as wasp, name as poison. To render anything denatures it. Stains it the color of render. This theory believes we yearn toward our names, whereas the former says our names yearn toward us.

Either way you want it, any way you undress it, you find desire pulsing at the center.

Either way, I am afraid to write my rapist's name.

*

When we meet, he is dressed in a green polo shirt and khaki shorts.

He says he is going to a friend's mother's funeral, he'll be back the next day.

He is letting me stay in his apartment, a one-bedroom that he shares with his best friend, but just until the friend can "find his own place."

Who dresses this way for a funeral? What kind of funeral is over-night? Why is the best friend in all the photographs in the apartment? These questions belong to some unknown realm of fact, the name of which I do not know.

He comes back early, while I am sleeping.

I am startled awake.

He is an excellent kisser.

*

Rape (v): To transport with delight, to enrapture. Obs.

*

Months later, months after we stop knowing each other, I am surprised to see him: At the grocery store in Pittsburgh, at a rest stop in Missouri, ordering a bourbon in a bar called Plush in Tucson, at a McDonald's in Cicero, New York. He strides down the frozen foods aisle in a pea coat. Down the sidewalk in boot-cut jeans. Across the room at a party, eyes dancing with too much bourbon. Always, shoulders squared and nonchalant. Time slows and quickens, behaving like one of those movie montages when the heroine sees her crush and suddenly the camera focuses yet hazes. I forget not how to exhale, but that I have breath in me at all. This is how I knew I was ravaged: Time has entered my blood stream, marching the rigor mortis minutes ahead in my arteries. I see him everywhere. He is everyman.

*

The first time we meet I stay with him for three nights over the Memorial Day holiday. During sex I say, "Fuck me harder" and he asks me to please be quiet, then puts his hand over my mouth when I am unwilling or incapable of obeying.

The first time we meet, we eat green tea ice cream for dessert, but only one scoop.

He lives in the same building as Dr. Ruth; I see her in the elevator but don't say a word. I imagine her listening to us on the other side of his wall, taking notes, holding up score cards.

His friend sleeps on the couch in the living room. He is chubby like me, with a handsome face. There's a picture of he and M. on the nightstand, dressed up as cowboys, sepia-toned. One night, the friend makes dinner for the three of us and M. goes out for more ice cream. The roommate turns to me: "Just FYI, buddy, I have been the constant in his life. I'm The Mother," he says.

The next day, after breakfast, The Mother asks, "Could I pass for twenty-eight?" with his computer open in front of him, his cell phone out to take a photo. "I don't think so," I say, contemplatively, trying to be honest. "But I'm actually really bad at the age game."

*

M. told me he was thirty-five.

Google told me he was forty-two.

Over green tea ice cream, I encourage him to Google himself so he can find the article that lists his real age. I want him to know I know, that I'm not stupid or shallow.

*

(I have never thought of art as revenge, myself as vindictive, but now I am afraid this is turning into retaliation. So what. Maybe modern writing would be better with a little more blood and flesh at stake. As Anne Lamott says, "If people wanted you to write warmly about them, they should have behaved better."

It's better that you know this now: Even if this was a story, I would not be the hero.)

The second time I visit, in August, I have the sense that I am the source of a fight between M. and The Mother.

M. and I have corresponded spottily. There is one long, lushly described email, recounting a run for miles alongside the Rhine. It is the letter I read when I want to believe there is solid land, not some airy kingdom of fluff and cloud between us. It ends with M. describing how he'd stripped off his clothes—not a stitch between him and the honest God—and jumped into the river, purified in blue.

But since he'd returned from Europe, I'd heard nothing: not a hello, certainly not an invitation. I only find myself in his apartment again by making up an excuse to be in the city. M. had agreed to one night. Which means The Mother was on the couch again.

In bed, M. says it's too bad I don't bareback, hesitating with an unopened condom balanced on his palm, gesturing towards me, as if it was an offering. A sacrifice.

I laugh and wag a finger no.

We are naked on his bed, he is above me, my legs against his chest, my ankles notched in the small dips of his well-defined biceps.

I say *Fuck me harder*. He says *Quiet*. Inserts four fingers into my mouth. Curls them around my bottom teeth. His other arm makes a bar against my legs and pushes them to my chest. The air flattens out of me. I want to but cannot say no.

The color of fire in my head. It lasts thirty seconds, maybe less, before he fills his condoms and collapses. I see myself from above this scene, a third person who knows something is wrong.

It takes a long time before the I I am can reenter itself.

*

For Christmas that year, at my parents' house in Indiana, my brother unwraps a present from my mother. A door hanger that says, *I Liked You Better Before I Knew You So Well*. Of course I love it, of course it makes me think of M., who is still the last person to have seen me naked. I liked you better when you were my fantasy, before you ruined how I composed you, demolished yourself with who you are.

*

Render. v. To describe, to name. To build under a single name all the things one can be.

Render. v. To rend apart, to tear apart, to shred into all the things one can be.

*

In the bathroom, there is a spot of blood swimming in the toilet. A bruise is starting to bloom on my chest.

He is lounging on his bed, one knee up, still naked. The windows are open. Nothing will make them wince.

I crawl in between his legs and begin sucking his flaccid dick until he's hard again. I kiss up his belly, his chest, bite his shoulder and growl into his ear, "Fuck me again." He struggles to come, but finally does, weakly, I note, his eyes closed the whole time. Thinking of some other body. This stupid one I'm in goes to sleep feeling victorious.

*

In the morning his face is innocent, asleep. I make breakfast, eggs scrambled with mozzarella and spinach. In the hallway, he says good morning through a yawn.

"I made coffee," I say. There may be too much *good morning* in my voice.

Then, a full waking in his eyes, he says, "Did I hurt you last night?" There is a half-smile parting his lips.

"You could never hurt me," I say, jerking my head toward the table.

We eat the eggs in silence.

I ask him if I can stay another day. He is annoyed, but agrees. We spend the day in separate rooms, composing our different scores. Later that night, we don't have sex. M., me, and The Mother crowd into the bed and watch something funny until we fall asleep.

*

Before school starts, I write him to say let's see each other more. I make a pitch—two weekends a month, until it stops being fun. He writes back, *I can't complicate my life right now.* Everything I knew but kept at bay comes hurtling in through the window.

For six months, I describe what happened to friends and say, "But I didn't tell him no."

It's not like I was raped, I say.

I am ashamed of all the needs living in my body that drove him away. All the drippy sentences I wrote to try to make him love me.

I stay celibate for six months.

I liked myself better before I knew me so well.

*

It takes another six months before I can use the word rape. Before I can wear the name *survivor*. Rape survivors are:

- Six times more likely to suffer from post-traumatic stress disorder

- Twenty-six times more likely to abuse drugs

- Four times more likely to contemplate suicide

Winter in upstate New York, snow piled up to the windows, my car stopped, everything overquiet, and I am watching an episode of *The Real Housewives of New Jersey* when I walk out of my body into the field of gleaming snow behind my house. A gun's weight pulls my hand down, the heaviest thing I will ever hold. I walk so easily through the drifts in my red sweatpants and gray t-shirt, out to the edge of the trees behind my house. I do not turn to face the road, but put the gun in my mouth, at first just to feel it split the lips, amazed at how the metal recognizes my teeth, telling them it is superior, and it is, I can't stop it from gaining access to the roof of my mouth where all the cold stops. I can't hear anything. The I I am recedes into the sound of snow laying down on snow. Then even that sound starts to echo into the imperceptible

—And when I come back into my body, to my self, the episode is over, and I am shaking from the cold that has entered me, the cold that has lived there without warning, without my noticing.

*

Sometimes I am in my bed, alone, thinking of well-defined pecs, the muscled arms, the ripples on the abdomen. I am bending space, bending him into a body that suits my need, making him into fact, into an object I can play with.

Until I see his eyes. A blue the color of flame. My hand stops, scalded, I'm embarrassed and looking for a washcloth.

This ritual, more nights than I care to admit. Starting the most private tenderness. And stopping it.

Or, worse, finishing because I could not stop touching the bruise of his memory.

*

That first night, alone in his apartment, we looked out the windows at the George Washington Bridge, lit from within its bracing, one long scintillant smear, visible from his view on the ninth floor. I told him about my favorite novel, *Another Country*, which opens with the main character, Rufus, jumping off that bridge. "That's why you love it?" he asked, appalled. I sputtered to explain. Death isn't more or less beautiful than any other banal pain we experience, he said to me.

Later, M. played a recording he made with a friend of his in an old English church. The sound was unlike anything I'd ever heard a piano make, a beauty so haunted and occasionally discordant it could not contain its reverberations. Each note bled over into the next two. M. explained they'd bent back the top of the old upright piano, exposing its catgut strings. The friend then sat at the bench, striking keys while M. laid on top of the piano, reaching down to dampen and pluck, changing the vibration by hand.

I think sometimes about the music. That the recording had a warning: key struck, string gripped tight. It became a lesson: when you are changed, you don't change back.

But neither do you stay the form he made.

*

Over dinner the last night I saw him—the night after he raped me—he says, "My greatest regret is that when I was a kid, as hard as I tried to seduce him, my uncle would not molest me." Twirling his pasta with his fork, staring at me, the most vulnerable I would ever see him.

*

Sometimes, when I tell people, they overlay my rape on top of what they know about me.

Sometimes the fact does not settle into the existing frame of me.

Sometimes the fact subsumes it, a too-heavy roof, and what I was splinters, the foundation of me buckles, I'm a ruin, uninhabitable because the fact takes up all the space someone has for what I am, the fact is so large a presence it is my self, or all the self the other person can allow.

I liked you better before I knew you so well.

*

1. Why didn't you file a police report?
2. How much breath does *no* take?

3. Do you think it's possible some part of you enjoyed it?

4. Why would you ever tell me this?

*

It's Christmas night, 2014. I am at my parents' house in southeast Indiana. My now-disabled father has gone to sleep; it's just my two brothers and me keeping my mother company.

CJ brings up a poem of mine that begins: "One August night a man will cook me dinner / and rape me in his bed." CJ wants to know: Is it true?

We are brothers who are not close. But he's asking for an intimacy I do not deny the people who have read the poem online, which is to say, complete strangers.

I feel strange to myself, again. It's true, I say.

And then, as always, it's truer.

My mother stops her conversation with Dustin. What's true, she wants to know.

CJ says, That your middle son was graped.

What, my mother says?

What? I say.

Graped? We speak together, in italics. We look at each other, heads cocked.

Drop the G, he says.

There is a pause, a subtraction added to the air.

Oh, my mother says, turning to me. That explains a lot about you.

What does it explain, I ask quietly. But no one answers.

What does it explain? Louder, and no one answers.

*

Render: Does my body absorb my experience? Is my body a repository of what happens to me, archive of transitive verbs?

Render: If my body dies, am I no longer raped?

Render: The fantasy about the man is made by the fantasy about the gun.

Reconcile: In cases where the offender is a friend of or acquaintance, an average of 71 percent of rapes go unreported.

Reconcile: In cases where the offender is a stranger, an average of 44 percent of rapes are not reported.

When the offender makes you a stranger to yourself, there is no form to fill out, no way to measure that alchemy.

No way to report the parts of you that go missing.

When the offender makes you a stranger to yourself, sometimes you (stranger) turn against you (familiar).

This is another way you learn to love your enemy.

*

Martin. His name is surprisingly dorky. It means a kind of songbird in the swallow family. Two syllables he overenunciates, making both syllables stressed. Mar

Tin. Two notes struck hard. A spondee, like heartbreak. Almost harmless. Derived from Mars, guardian of soldiers and farmers. Father of the Roman Empire.

*

I liked you better when you were the name I knew for you.

I liked you better when you were an unreverberating fact.

I could stand in the middle of you and everywhere I looked the field made sense.

When you were revealed to me, you changed.

You became a fruit the color of bruise, picked and barreled. Someone's feet trod you into someone else's fermented pleasure.

I liked you better when you weren't broken into.

I liked you better in the well I would not peer down into, before I saw your face down there in the dim light.

I liked you better when I did not have to face my own face, diminished.

Before I saw it was cruelty that bonds us together.

Some names have been changed.

My First Time:

> The word *faggot* dates from the end of the fourteenth century.
> According to the *Oxford English Dictionary*, it means "a bundle of
> sticks, twigs, or small branches of trees bound together," as in this
> sentence by Bartholomew de Glanville, in his *De Proprietatibus
> Rerum*, translated by John Trevisa: "Thornes ... ben bounde in
> faggottes ... and brent in ouens."

The Ends of Terror:

> President Dwight D. Eisenhower signed Executive Order 10450 in
> 1953, setting security standards for federal employees and barring
> homosexuals from federal employ. The EO caused the firing of
> approximately five thousand homosexuals from federal employment;
> this included private contractors and military personnel. The EO
> stayed on paper and in effect for forty-two years, until President Bill
> Clinton rescinded the order and instituted what became known as
> the "Don't ask, don't tell" policy for the military.

Hitler: The Psychopathic God was written by Robert G.L. Waite, Professor Emeritus at Williams College, and published in June 1977, six months after I was born.

Joan Collins originated the role of Alexis Carrington in *Dynasty*'s second season, sweeping in to a courtroom in a black-and-white suit, a wide-brimmed white hat, and oversized sunglasses. Collins's Nolan Miller-designed wardrobe cost the studio a reported $35,000 per week.

Prophecy:

Stetson University ended its affiliation with the Florida Baptist Convention in 1995, the year after I entered as a first-year political science and English double-major.

Chris Rock says he got the idea for his acclaimed documentary *Good Hair* when his young daughter asked him, "Daddy, why don't I have good hair?" In the film, the Rev. Al Sharpton says, "We wear our economic oppression on our heads."

According to Volusia County court records, my paternal grandfather exposed his genitalia to an undercover officer. Adjudication was withheld; he paid thirty dollars monthly for six months and was given supervised probation, in addition to mandatory STD testing. The exposure occurred on November 21, 1991, in Valentine Park, a place where my brothers and I used to play soccer when we were kids.

In the biblical story of Samson and Delilah, she is a kind of spy for the other side. She asks him the source of his power several times, and he gives decoy answers, only to wake each morning with Delilah having acted to render him powerless. Why didn't he see her working against him? Did he think it was some courting gesture? Of course Samson must pay for his surrender to desire's thrall: first, he is blinded, and then he is abandoned by God.

Suicide Memorabilia:

Madonna's hit "Borderline" was released on her eponymous debut album in 1984.

A Scorpio makes a less-than-desirable match for an Aries like my mother.

Before my mother decided to move in with Jesse in Dallas, my parents took turns reading a book called *Final Exit* in front of me and Dustin. Like, "Oh this? Just some light reading we picked up at Half-Price Books."

My father suffered a stroke in Houston on July 4, 2003. My mother returned for the ensuing months. When she finally left Jesse in 2006, she moved with my father and my older brother to Indiana. My mother stayed married to Jesse for ten more years.

Adventures in Old Lady Land:

> You can watch the OB tampon commercial here: https://www.you-tube.com/watch?v=mVnvLwEOqJw

> You can watch anti-gay activist Anita Bryant rant against homosex-uals and receive a pie in the face here: https://www.youtube.com/watch?v=dS91gT3XT_A

My AIDS:

> Martha Wash was one half of Two Tons o' Fun, who renamed themselves The Weather Girls in 1982, the same year they released the multiplatinum hit "It's Raining Men." Wash pushed successfully for legislation that mandated the listing of vocal credits on CDs and music videos after being uncredited and thus denied royalties for her work on the megahit "Gonna Make You Sweat (Everybody Dance Now)."

> You can view and search the entire fifty-four-ton AIDS Memorial Quilt online at http://www.aidsquilt.org/view-the-quilt/search-the-quilt

> Brownstown, Indiana was named for General Jacob Brown who served in the War of 1812. The 2010 census records just under three thousand people living in Brownstown; 98.3 percent of them are white.

> The first male "scream queen" is generally recognized to be Mark Patton, who played Jesse Walsh in *Nightmare on Elm Street: Freddy's Revenge*. In the movie, Krueger possesses Jesse's body. In real life, Patton is openly gay and HIV positive.

Be Destroyed:

> The website of my parents' former employer boasts that they have "over 6 million sonobuoys deployed to the United States and foreign customers .... Sparton continues to serve as a vital supplier to these militaries with the most effective antisubmarine warfare sensor capability."

> My mother recently said she'd like her and my father's ashes spread out on the water, within view of the Aku Tikki Lounge.

> Weston, Florida is the westernmost city in Broward County and was named by *Money* magazine as the best city to live in Florida.

In Lieu of Drugs:

> Narcotics Anonymous: https://www.na.org

> According to The Treatment Center, an addiction recovery program center, the most commonly overused drugs in the Pittsburgh area are cocaine, heroin, prescription pills, and methamphetamine. Most overdose deaths in Allegheny County are due to heroin and cocaine, according to the July 2016 unclassified report issued by the DEA.

> The "While You're Using" list can be found at http://www.tweaker. org/life/tweaktips/takeoff.html.

I Liked You Better Before I Knew You So Well:

"It [exile] is not so much a rending to be separated from your own, to
be rendered ineffective as it were; no, the pain is in being disconnect-
ed from normalcy and eventually to become the living experience of
the fact that exiled memory is the slow art of forgetting the color of
fire," writes Breyten Breytenback in his essay, "The Long March from
Hearth to Heart."

Statistics regarding rape survivors are taken from the RISE website,
http://www.riseslo.org.org. RISE is a nonprofit organization that
provides intervention and treatment serices to survivors of sexual and
intimate partner violence. All services are provided confidentially and
at low or no cost.

Definitions taken from the *Oxford English Dictionary*.

In *Bird by Bird*, Anne Lamott writes, "You own everything that happened to you. Tell your stories. If people wanted you to write warmly
about them, they should have behaved better."

The rape survivor list can be found at http://www.riseslo.org/facts_
about_sexual_assault.php.

ACKNOWLEDGEMENTS

I want to express my gratitude to the editors of the following literary journals that published some of these essays (occasionally in slightly different versions):

Alaska Quarterly	Be Destroyed
Bennington Review	I Liked You Better Before I Knew You So Well
Bellingham Review	My AIDS
Cimarron Review	Adventures in Old Lady Land
CutBank	Prophecy
James White Review	My First Time
Pebble Lake Review	Suicide Memorabilia
Redivider	The Ends of Terror
Story Quarterly	In Lieu of Drugs

James Allen Hall is also the author of a book of poems, *Now You're the Enemy*, which won awards from the Texas Institute of Letters, the Lambda Literary Foundation, and the Fellowship of Southern Writers. He teaches at Washington College on Maryland's Eastern Shore and divides his time between Chestertown and Baltimore.